Red, White, and Columbia Blue:

Chasing the Dream with the 1979 Houston Oilers

Written and compiled by: Jackson Michael

Mission Hills Media, New Braunfels, TX 78132

Copyright 2020 by 11 Productions. All rights reserved.

Table of Contents

PREGAME PREFACE The Most Famous Play in Oiler History   7

PART 1 PREGAME INTRODUCTIONS   13
    CHAPTER 1 A Recap of 1978 and the Off-Season   14
    CHAPTER 2 1979 Training Camp and the Preseason   20

PART 2 COURAGE OUT OF THE GATE   31
    CHAPTER 3 Week 1 – AT WASHINGTON   32
    CHAPTER 4 Week 2 – AT PITTSBURGH   37
    CHAPTER 5 Week 3 – HOME VS. KANSAS CITY   42
    CHAPTER 6 Week 4 – AT CINCINNATI   46
    CHAPTER 7 Week 5 – HOME VS. CLEVELAND   54

PART 3 TWISTS AND TURNS ALONG KIRBY DRIVE   59
    CHAPTER 8 Week 6 – HOME VS. ST. LOUIS   60
    CHAPTER 9 Week 7 – AT BALTIMORE   63
    CHAPTER 10 Week 8 – AT SEATTLE   67
    CHAPTER 11 Bum And His Crew   71

PART 4 DIGGING DEEPER — 81

    CHAPTER 12 Week 9 – HOME VS. NEW YORK JETS — 82

    CHAPTER 13 Week 10 – AT MIAMI — 87

    CHAPTER 14 Week 11 – HOME VS. OAKLAND — 94

    CHAPTER 15 Week 12 – HOME VS. CINCINNATI — 98

    CHAPTER 16 Week 13 – AT DALLAS — 102

    CHAPTER 17 Week 14 – AT CLEVELAND — 118

    CHAPTER 18 Rockin' at the Astrodome — 123

    CHAPTER 19 Week 15 – HOME VS. PITTSBURGH — 130

    CHAPTER 20 Week 16 – HOME VS. PHILADELPHIA — 144

PART 5 THE EXTRA MILE: THE PLAYOFFS — 151

    CHAPTER 21 Wildcard Round – HOME VS. DENVER — 153

    CHAPTER 22 Divisional Round – AT SAN DIEGO — 167

    CHAPTER 23 1979 AFC Championship Game — 184

    CHAPTER 24 The Renfro Play — 201

    CHAPTER 25 The Last Quarter Mile — 209

    CHAPTER 26 The Journey Domeward — 213

PART 6 A NEW DECADE AND NEW DESTINATIONS — 225

    CHAPTER 27 The Sun Rises and Also Sets — 226

PART 7 POSTGAME WRAP UP — 231

    CHAPTER 28 Reflecting on the Scrapbook — 232

Acknowledgements — 238

About the Author — 240

PREGAME PREFACE
The Most Famous Play in Oiler History

The most famous scene of our story took place on the frosty stage of Three Rivers Stadium in Pittsburgh. The 1979 AFC Championship Game approached the end of the third quarter as the Houston Oilers and Pittsburgh Steelers relentlessly pushed their limits in separate quests for the ultimate treasure – a trip to sunny Pasadena, California and top billing in the NFL's championship bout, Super Bowl 14.

The Steelers' grip on a 17-10 lead precariously slipped as Houston pulled its way inside the Pittsburgh 10-yard line. Oiler quarterback Dan Pastorini called a play, broke the huddle, and sauntered to the line of scrimmage.

Pastorini surveyed the landscape of the Steelers' Steel Curtain defense. He changed the play call through an audible. He took the snap, took two quick steps back, and fired a pass into history.

Houston receiver Mike Renfro leapt over Pittsburgh defensive back Ron Johnson. Renfro snatched the ball from the air, planted one foot in bounds, and dragged the other across a slim, green patch of end zone. He rolled and slid on his back. He extended his left arm into the air and his index finger waved the #1 sign. His right arm cradled the football against his chest.

Millions of NFL fans who watched the game on television assumed they had just witnessed a game-tying touchdown completed within the blink of an eye.

The game's officials, however, weren't so sure. In fact, the officials seemed so uncertain about what happened that nobody signaled touchdown, incomplete, or even time for a coffee break.

Renfro stood up, waved his arms, and screamed at the officials to make a call.

The officials called a meeting instead. That prompted Steelers' owner Art Rooney to reportedly grumble and compare the officiating crew to the United Nations.

The zebra-striped group herded themselves near the goal post. At first, players from both teams expressed their opinions. Teammates shoved those players away to avoid penalties.

The time the officials took to discuss the play gave broadcasting network NBC a platform to show viewers two replay angles. The replays confirmed in many fans' minds that the Oilers scored a touchdown.

Moreover, it gave announcers Dick Enberg and Merlin Olsen plenty of time to also conclude that Renfro scored. They theorized that the officials might not have seen the play. Enberg noted that situations like this might be resolved by officials viewing a replay. The NFL, however, had yet to adopt instant replay for reviewing calls.

Referee Jim Tunney finally broke the official's huddle and called the pass incomplete.

No touchdown. No tie going into the fourth quarter between arguably the two best teams in football. The Oilers settled for a field goal and the Steelers kept their lead, 17-13.

Pittsburgh went on to win the game and Super Bowl 14.

The "Renfro Play" and the officials' indecision intensified both fans' and television networks' pleas for instant replay to confirm or reverse close calls. The result of the play left clouds of question marks floating through NFL history.

What if Dan Pastorini's pass to Mike Renfro was ruled a touchdown? What if the Oilers and Steelers were tied going into the fourth quarter? Would the Oilers have ridden their newly found momentum to victory, or would the Steelers still have outscored Houston by double digits in the fourth quarter?

Definitive answers escape us like Walter Payton escaped defensive lines. Reality always lands on the pass being ruled incomplete, an Oiler field goal, and the Steelers winning both the 1979 AFC Championship Game and Super Bowl 14.

Sports history often condenses games into one or two quick plays. Those condensed stories pass down from generation to generation and from history book to history book. Points of the narrative fall away like forgotten heirlooms stored in the attic. People remember a few major characters and perhaps a couple of moments. The rest of the story drifts away into dusty, forgotten corners of time.

The 1979 Houston Oilers season often gets condensed into one play – "The Pass That Launched a Thousand Replays." The play counted for nothing except a second-and-goal and a single digit added to the incomplete column of Dan Pastorini's stat sheet.

The jubilant homecoming for the Oilers and the rest of the 1979 playoffs sit like yellowed photographs stored between the pages of large scrapbooks used more for décor than reminiscing. The Renfro Play stands as the cover image of the season.

The full story of the 1979 Houston Oilers, however, involves far deeper stories than what's been passed on through the years. Underneath such layers lay stories of triumph through adversity, a coaching staff led by Bum Phillips that brought out the best in each player, and a team that never quit.

The 1979 Oilers – the pinnacle of the "Luv Ya Blue" era – might have fielded the most talented and resilient team in franchise history. The team became like family both amongst themselves and with the city of Houston.

Nineteen seventy-nine was not just a gusher of a football season. Houston's economy also boomed, and for fans and players alike, the memories remain priceless.

Football parallels life in many ways. As the members of the 1979 Houston Oilers represented a city and a franchise, they also embarked on a steadfast journey toward the dream of winning Super Bowl 14. Although the ultimate objective eluded powerful blocks and outstretched hands, the 1979 season forced a group of men to overcome both inward and outward trials, challenged individuals and a team to discover their true limits, and yielded treasures still enjoyed today in the hearts of those who lived it, witnessed it, and shared in the adventure.

Now, long after the last pom-pom has been waved, the final news story published on thin newsprint, and the lights dimmed on the Astrodome in favor of the shinier gloss of a modern stadium, perhaps a clearer inventory of the 1979 Oilers accomplishments can be harvested with the ancient tools of time and hindsight.

PART 1
PREGAME INTRODUCTIONS

CHAPTER 1

A Recap of 1978 and the Off-Season

In 1978, the Houston Oilers scaled the NFL's cliffs all the way to the AFC Championship Game, the furthest the franchise had climbed since 1962 when the Oilers made the American Football League Championship Game.

Sportswriters dubbed the 1978 AFC Championship as, "World War 3" prior to the game. The Oilers and Steelers played physical football, especially against each other. Bum Phillips said, "time to get the bandages out" each time the two played. Their regular season matchup in the Astrodome produced so many injuries that it was called, "The Bandage Bowl." The two division rivals readied themselves for their third showdown of the year, and many experts believed the game stood as the true Super Bowl and would ultimately decide the NFL's champion.

The 1978 American Football Conference Championship Game didn't live up to the hype. Pittsburgh's Steel Curtain defense and poor weather conditions easily crushed the Oilers in an icy mix of turnovers and a second-quarter meltdown. The battle and the war basically ended before halftime, as the Steelers led 31-3 at the break. The final score was 34-5.

The Houston Oilers' 1978 season brought the arrival of rookie running back Earl Campbell. The team traded four draft choices and tight end Jimmie Giles to Tampa Bay for the draft's first-overall pick and the right to select Campbell.

The deal wasn't easy to pull off. Other teams, such as the Los Angeles Rams, dearly wanted Campbell. Oilers owner Bud Adams called Buccaneers owner Hugh Culverhouse and pleaded with him to trade the pick to Houston. Adams told Culverhouse that Campbell grew up in Texas and should play pro ball there. Culverhouse said he would talk to head coach John McKay but didn't sound too impressed. A few days later, Culverhouse called Adams back and said that he decided that trading the pick to Houston was the right thing to do. Campbell would wear the Columbia blue of the Houston Oilers.

Campbell earned legendary football status in Texas even before donning an Oiler uniform. His high school (John Tyler in Tyler, Texas) won the state football championship in 1973. They even won the championship game in the Astrodome. Campbell scored the game-winning touchdown, rushed for over 160 yards, and also starred at linebacker. Earl later won the Heisman Trophy at the University of Texas and vaulted the Longhorns to the brink of a national championship.

Before Campbell joined the Oilers, most NFL defenses focused on stopping Houston's dynamic combination of quarterback Dan Pastorini and game-breaking receiver Ken Burrough.

Burrough caught 23 touchdowns from 1975 through 1977. Eighteen of those touchdowns went for more than 40 yards. Burrough led the NFL in receiving yards in 1975 and made two Pro Bowls. Word circulated that if you stopped Pastorini and Burrough, you likely stopped the Oilers.

Earl Campbell spun those words into outdated playbook technology in 1978. He led the NFL in rushing yards and was named Offensive Player of the Year. He proclaimed his greatness to the nation against the revered Miami Dolphins defense on *Monday Night Football*, as he rushed for nearly 200 yards and scored 4 touchdowns.

That game also showcased the Houston Oiler fans as 50,000 pom-poms waved and fight songs blared from the Astrodome's loudspeakers. Pro football hadn't seen anything like Oiler fans, and modern defenses hadn't seen anything like Earl Campbell. Campbell's powerful running forced defenses to respect the Oilers' rushing attack. Pastorini found a good friend in the play-action pass as a result and he posted a career high in passing yards.

That 1978 Monday night game against Miami stood as one of the most important victories in a year that produced a 10-6 record. The 35-30 triumph pushed Houston's record to 8-4 and proved that a Week 8 *Monday Night Football* win at Pittsburgh was no fluke.

Another huge regular season win in 1978 came in Week 11 at New England. The Patriots, a team many predicted would win a championship, had won their last seven games, and owned a sparkling 8-2 record.

New England jumped out to a 23-0 lead before Houston finally got on the scoreboard late in the first half. Oilers Head Coach Bum Phillips didn't say much to the team at halftime.

Defensive end Andy Dorris remembers what Phillips said and how the Oilers felt in those moments.

"Bum called us into the locker room and said, 'Okay, we don't have much of a chance in this game so let's just go out there and have some fun. We'll pick up the pieces when we get back to Houston.'"

Dorris then commented on the team's mood after Phillips' statement. "And everybody in the locker room went, 'Holy cow. We're letting him down.'"

After the game, Ken Burrough told the *Houston Chronicle* that quarterback Dan Pastorini looked around the huddle and told his teammates to believe in him. Burrough stated that Pastorini shouted a similar message to the defense while the Patriots had the ball. Pastorini told the defense to believe that the offense owned the firepower to come back.

The defense held. The team believed.

Burrough said in wire reports that the feeling turned infectious. Fullback Rob Carpenter scored a second touchdown and made a critical first down on a fake field goal. Campbell added another touchdown on the ground. Rich Caster's touchdown reception put the Oilers ahead. Veteran defensive back Willie Alexander snatched a crucial interception. The defense completely shut down the Patriots offense in the second half.

The Oilers rallied and topped New England in Foxboro, 26-23.

That game provided the Oilers with a confidence-building cornerstone against adversity. It was a team win. That game and the Monday night victories against Pittsburgh and Miami demonstrated that the Oilers could stand with the NFL's best teams and win.

The playoffs furthered the point, as the wildcard Oilers upset both Miami and New England on the road.

Against Miami, both Ken Burrough and tight end Mike Barber each collected over 100 yards receiving. Earl Campbell and Tim Wilson combined for over 160 yards rushing.

In the playoff against New England, Pastorini fired a long touchdown to Burrough and two touchdowns to Barber before the Patriots had a chance to ready their cannons. Earl Campbell added almost 120 yards rushing in the 31-14 Oiler onslaught.

Then came Pittsburgh and the sobering 34-5 defeat.

A huge homecoming eased the pain. The team busses went directly from the airport to the Astrodome. Tens of thousands filled the Dome to welcome the team back. The players and coaches couldn't believe it. What other city would euphorically cheer a team that just got hammered by a hated divisional rival in a championship game?

Eventually, however, the crushing pain of defeat returned. The team sat one game away from playing in Super Bowl 13 and the Oiler playoff rocket sputtered on takeoff.

Two weeks later, Pittsburgh won their third Super Bowl in five years. That made the Steelers the only team at the time to have won three Super Bowls.

Dan Pastorini took the AFC Championship loss especially hard. Early in his career, he suffered through back-to-back seasons which produced only one victory each. Defensive lines beat him to within inches of his career.

He played in the 1978 AFC Championship wearing a flak jacket – the first of its kind – to protect three broken ribs. A doctor administered two dozen painkilling shots before and during the game. He endured the shots, twelve before each game and twelve at halftime, for the last three regular season games of 1978 and throughout the playoffs.

That kind of toughness proved him a leader in his teammates' eyes, as defensive end Andy Dorris stated.

"He was extremely tough," Dorris said. "I saw him take about fifteen shots before the Miami game in the playoffs. Everybody saw it, there was no pulled curtain. He was not going to be taken out of that game. He was going to play. And from that point on I said, 'Dan, you're my quarterback.'"

Pastorini did not only feel the physical pain of the broken ribs and the emotional pain of losing. He also felt stinging criticism. People vandalized his car and home at times throughout his career. As a quarterback, Pastorini took painful shots from defensive linemen, painful shots from doctors, and hurtful blows on newsprint from columnists and letters to the editor.

As Pastorini dealt with the loss in the 1978 AFC Championship, he battled inner emotions and at times blamed himself for the Oilers' poor showing at Pittsburgh. He met with Bum Phillips in Bum's office during the off-season.

Pastorini explained that he felt like he might have lost that game for the Oilers and that he loved the team and Phillips too much to hold things back. Pastorini told Phillips to trade him if thought he was the problem keeping the Oilers out of the Super Bowl.

Phillips told Pastorini that he put too much pressure on himself and that he didn't want to trade him. Phillips then told Pastorini to focus on the upcoming 1979 season. He said the two could check back after the season was over. If Dan felt the same way after the season was over, Bum told him he'd trade him anywhere he wanted to go.

Pastorini owned considerable trade value. Teams around the league recognized Pastorini's arm as one of the strongest in football. His arm always represented a long-gain threat against defenses.

That powerful throwing arm of Dan Pastorini, the arm that allowed him to rifle a football through double coverage into his receiver's jersey numbers, collapsed a few weeks later. He opened a door to a department store and felt his arm buckle and completely lose strength.

He went home and picked up a football. The same arm that once threw a ball over 80 yards in an ABC network competition between star NFL quarterbacks -- much further than any other competitor – could now barely throw the ball at all.

The toll of the painkilling shots had apparently damaged a nerve that controls shoulder movement.

Pastorini wondered if his career might be over.

CHAPTER 2

1979 Training Camp and the Preseason

Head coach Bum Phillips started training camp early for rookies and free agents. They reported on July 3rd, the earliest date ever for an Oiler squad. He said that the early start gave them a better shot at making the team after the NFL changed schedule formats for the 1978 season.

Before 1978, teams played 6 preseason games and 14 regular season games. In 1978, regular season games increased to 16, while preseason games reduced to 4.

The Oilers drafted to increase their pass rush and selected defensive linemen Mike Stensrud and Jesse Baker with their first two picks, both in the second round.

The NFL draft wasn't televised like it is today. The Oilers called Stensrud while he was out having a few beers with friends. His wife answered the team's phone call.

She made her way to the local bar and told Stensrud that the Oilers wanted him at a press conference in Houston the following day. That's how a second-round draft pick learned he was drafted by an NFL team in 1979.

Other Oiler draftees that year included two players from the University of Oklahoma: running back Kenny King and linebacker Daryl Hunt. Houston also picked up Carter Hartwig and Rich Ellender.

The incoming free agents weren't star players signed away from other NFL teams. NFL players did not enjoy that type of free agency until the 1990s. The free agents who attended the Oiler training camp were players cut by other teams, undrafted players offered a tryout, and occasionally players who had played in the Canadian Football League (CFL).

Defensive back Vernon Perry was one such player who played in the CFL. He snatched 9 interceptions in one season for the Montreal Alouettes. That total would have led the Oilers in interceptions in 1978, and it caught the attention of Houston's coaching staff.

The Oilers used the 3-4 defense, modeled after the defense Don Shula's Miami Dolphins employed during their undefeated season of 1972. The defense featured three defensive linemen up front and four linebackers.

Houston head coach Bum Phillips, defensive coordinator Ed Biles, and defensive line coach Wade Phillips planned to utilize a 4-3 defensive scheme on certain passing downs in 1979. They hoped a fourth defensive lineman would increase pressure on quarterbacks, leading to higher sack and interception totals. The staff hoped Baker and Stensrud could play on the four-man front.

The Oiler coaching staff's main mission, however, was to win the 1979 AFC championship to earn the right to play in Super Bowl 14. The staff knew that the road to Super Bowl 14 crossed through Pittsburgh, and Bum Phillip's crew focused their strategy on melting the Steel Curtain.

"The emphasis was really on trying to figure out a way that we could beat Pittsburgh," Ed Biles said. "It was that simple but not easy because there weren't many changes in their lineup."

Although knocking out the reigning champion Steelers was easier said than done, the Oilers split their regular season games with Pittsburgh in 1977 and 1978. Those wins earned the Steelers' respect, especially since Houston was the only team to beat Pittsburgh at Three Rivers Stadium in 1978.

In fact, the Oilers were the only AFC Central opponent to win at Pittsburgh since Three Rivers Stadium opened in 1970. They did it twice. One win at Pittsburgh came in 1974 under head coach Sid Gillman with Bum Phillips at defensive coordinator and several current players in the starting lineup. The other win at Pittsburgh came in 1978.

In 1979, Bum Phillips' mandatory training camp arrival date for veterans was July 18th. Many veterans reported earlier. Excitement surrounded the Oiler camp at Angelo State University in San Angelo, Texas. Tight end Mike Barber said he remembers a winning feeling floating through summer's thick air, and higher fan attendance at practices.

Players often worked off-season jobs in those years. An NFL salary wasn't enough to pay the bills for most players, and it certainly wasn't enough to set one for life. Most players worked jobs in preparation for a second career after football ended. Still, Barber believes the exhilaration of 1978, highlighted with the Domecoming, inspired a record participation in the team's off-season training program.

Billy "White Shoes" Johnson stated that the team found confidence in the fact that Bum Phillips didn't change much for the new season. The 1979 Oilers placed their steps on the same foundation that brought them to the brink of Super Bowl 13 in the 1978 season.

Veterans knew their assignments. They also knew their teammates understood their own assignments. Players could be players and just play. They reacted instinctively rather than needing to think about which way to move.

The Oilers three-man defensive line totaled over 30 years of NFL experience. Future Hall of Famers Elvin Bethea and Curley Culp each lined up for their twelfth season, and defensive end Andy Dorris entered his seventh.

Bethea became the team's longest tenured player in history that season. He also held the franchise record for most consecutive games played. He led the team in sacks in 1978. His strength and quickness made him sturdy against the run.

Culp, the exceptional defensive tackle acquired from Kansas City, excelled at more than football. He also won the 1967 NCAA national heavyweight wrestling championship at Arizona State. Offensive lines double- and triple-teamed him on nearly every play. Culp was paramount to the 3-4 defense's success. He proved himself a rock for the Oilers where lesser men would have failed.

Dorris toiled on second-division teams in St. Louis, New Orleans, and Seattle before arriving on Bum Phillips' doorstep in 1977. He dedicated himself to becoming a better ballplayer over the off-season, following a weight program a former teammate shared with him.

Early in camp, Bum Phillips stood with a reporter in a tower above the practice field. Phillips proudly pointed out linebacker Robert Brazile. Phillips compared Brazile to a machine and noted that Robert wouldn't slow down even on the sidelines.

Brazile credited his work ethic to his college career at Jackson State under coach Bob Hill and with his Jackson State teammate Walter Payton.

"If you know the history of any guy who came from Jackson State, then you know we worked hard at Jackson State," Brazile said. "I think the key to that was Mr. Walter Payton. Walter was a guy that never stopped working out."

Robert added that Payton worked so hard that Coach Hill would joke, "We need to end this meeting by 9 o'clock so Walter can get back to working out."

Brazile said that he and Payton never felt that they did enough, owing their bodies the "ultimate push" when they had the opportunity. Brazile also gave his teammates the ultimate push at every chance.

Gregg Bingham lined up with Brazile at linebacker. The Purdue graduate commanded the defense, working as the defensive signal caller from his middle linebacker position. At that point, he had led the Oilers in tackles and assists for each of his seven NFL seasons. As dependable as the Houston humidity, he had started every game since being drafted by Houston in the fourth round of the 1973 NFL Draft.

On the offensive side, receiver Ken Burrough stood out not only for his playmaking ability but also for his jersey number – double zero. The number led to his nickname, "Double-0." Kenny acquired the number in college.

"Two guys wore 00 at Texas Southern before me and they went pro but when I went to my locker and saw 00, I thought it was a joke." Burrough remembered. "I said, 'I'm not going to wear 00.'"

Burrough added, "The coach was Clifford Paul, who didn't even play the radio. He said, 'You're either going to be double something or double nothing! Put that jersey on and shut up. And you better be out there on that field first!' That's the greatest thing that's probably happened for me as far as that jersey is concerned."

Burrough suffered through many losing seasons early in his career. The Saints drafted him in the first round of the 1970 NFL Draft. The team won only two games that year. The Oilers traded for Burrough and soon suffered back-to-back 1-13 seasons.

Burrough relished in the possibilities that 1979 offered the Houston Oilers and the dream of reaching Super Bowl 14.

"Every football player would like to win a Super Bowl. And coming into camp has always been exciting for me," Burrough said.

Billy "White Shoes" Johnson sparkled as both a receiver and kick returner. He joined the Oilers as a 15th-round pick in 1974 from Division 3 Widener University. From 1974 through 1977, he finished in the NFL's top 10 in all-purpose yards, led the NFL in punt returns for touchdowns twice, and led the NFL in kickoff returns for touchdowns once. He played in only a handful of games in 1978 due to a serious knee injury. He entered 1979 fully recovered and confident.

Like Johnson, receiver Mike Renfro returned to camp after a knee injury knocked him out of action. Renfro showed promise as a rookie in 1978 and came from good stock – his father Ray Renfro won championships with the Cleveland Browns during the 1950s. Renfro still needed a few more weeks to heal but was expected to fully recover and play.

Rich Caster came over from the Jets in 1978 and was the type of player Bum Phillips loved, as he could play both receiver and tight end without taking up two roster spots. He returned to camp after a solid 1978 campaign.

"I joined the club the year before through a trade from the Jets in 1978," Caster said. "I had a pretty good season my first year down there and was looking forward to the 1979 season, my second year there. We had Earl Campbell again and we thought that we could only get better from the year before."

The jewel of the offense, of course, was running back Earl Campbell. In 1978, he was the first rookie to lead the NFL in rushing since the legendary Jim Brown in 1957. Campbell gained the nickname, "The Tyler Rose" from a college teammate, and quickly became a thorn in the side of NFL defenses.

A punishing runner, Campbell tagged bruising hits on star NFL linebackers Isiah Robertson and Thomas "Hollywood" Henderson. He racked up over 1,400 yards as a rookie and earned honors for Rookie of the Year and the Associated Press' Offensive Player of the Year. Furthermore, Campbell perfectly fit into Houston and Bum Phillips' philosophy both on and off the field. He was a Texas native with strong values and a devotion to family.

Quarterback Dan Pastorini grew up in Northern California. Sports ran in his blood. His father played organized baseball with Joe DiMaggio and was also offered a contract by the New York Yankees. Dan himself shined in baseball and was drafted by the New York Mets. He built arm strength and accuracy as a kid by tossing rocks on his family's 10-acre property.

Pastorini had worked tirelessly through the off-season in a diligent attempt to rebuild his arm strength. He wore a special pad under his jersey with a wing plate that helped hold his arm in place when throwing. The situation was far from ideal but Pastorini compensated and made it work.

The Oiler preseason schedule officially started August 2, but injuries hampered the Oilers before their game with the St. Louis Cardinals. The Oilers lost two starting offensive linemen early in camp. George Reihner, a man who made the NFL's all-rookie team in 1977, went down with a knee injury and missed most of 1979.

A more serious injury occurred to starting left tackle Greg Sampson. He suffered a severe head injury that required emergency surgery. His promising career ended as a result.

Houston split their first two preseason games. A blocked punt and several mistakes on the left side left vacant by the injuries to Reihner and Sampson contributed to a loss against the Jets.

A few days later, the Oilers traded their first- and sixth-round picks in the 1980 draft to the New England Patriots for All-Pro tackle Leon Gray. Gray received the news right after his wife gave birth to their first child.

Gray and guard Conway Hayman soon shored up Houston's troubled left side. Hayman came to the Oilers in 1975 and had started at both guard and tackle. The league limited rosters to 45 players, so Hayman's versatility proved especially valuable.

Bum felt like the Oilers fielded good athletes in the past, but now it felt more like a team than a group of players. Phillips worked hard to achieve that. He scheduled regular team events to build camaraderie and a family-like atmosphere. The players appreciated it and the functions made football more enjoyable. For example, Phillips set aside one night a week during camp for fun, something other teams didn't do.

Center Carl Mauck recalled those nights. "We had some great times in training camp out in San Angelo. Wednesday night was the night we drank beer and played dominoes and cards as a whole team, the coaches and players. He believed you had to get to know everybody. The coaches needed to get to know the players and the players needed to get to know the coaches."

Phillips' philosophy was simple. He believed one would fight harder for someone they regarded as family rather than just a friend or teammate. He was right, and the players saw the highest member of the family as Bum Phillips. They not only fought for each other, they fought for him.

Phillips carried two quarterbacks, Pastorini and backup Gifford Nielsen. In college, Nielsen had led the nation in passing yards and touchdowns at BYU. The Oilers picked him up in the third round of the 1978 NFL Draft. He only threw a handful of passes during his rookie season but led the Oilers to a preseason victory over the Dallas Cowboys.

The Oilers and Cowboys were scheduled to meet again in the third week of the 1979 preseason. Pastorini missed the Jets game due to injury but was expected to play against Dallas. His recovery, however, hit a speed bump.

On the very last day of training camp, on his very last throw, Pastorini tore a pectoral muscle. He watched the Cowboys preseason game from the sidelines in street clothes. Dallas won the game 16-13, but the Oilers had a second chance with the Cowboys scheduled during the regular season on Thanksgiving Day.

The Oilers described Pastorini's injury as a sore arm. It was occasionally called a viral infection. They hinted at nerve and shoulder damage but granting full information to the press was a sensitive issue.

The more the press knew, the more the public knew, and the more the public knew, the more opponents knew about Pastorini's condition. The league viewed his arm as a weapon that could strike a 50-yard touchdown to Kenny Burrough at any moment. Defenses needed to respect that possibility and adjusted their defenses accordingly. They couldn't just stack up against Earl Campbell or cover receivers short.

Pastorini played the first half in the final preseason game at New Orleans. He played well, throwing a touchdown pass to Billy Johnson. A second touchdown to Johnson was called back due to a penalty. The Saints kicked a game-winning field goal at the end to finalize Houston's preseason record at 1-3.

The Saints game marked Leon Gray's first in an Oiler uniform. Gray likely stood as the most notable of the team's new players. Defense back Vernon Perry and draftee Jesse Baker also stood poised to contribute.

Phillips said that he'd never seen a team with so many preseason injuries. The season wouldn't wait on the Oilers getting healthy before starting, however, and three of the first four games were on the road.

Houston needed tough resolve. Multiple early losses can send seasons into turmoil and leave teams with unsurmountable tasks by mid-season.

The Oilers' first task was to win early, often, and on the road. Failing this test would likely prevent them from making a playoff run down the stretch, especially considering they faced one of the league's toughest schedules.

PART 2
COURAGE OUT OF THE GATE

CHAPTER 3
Week 1 – AT WASHINGTON

Twenty-eight NFL teams lined the starting gate to kick off the 1979 season. Teams holding a real chance to win included the reigning champion Steelers, the defending NFC champion Cowboys, the Miami Dolphins, and the Oakland Raiders.

Each of those teams appeared on the Oilers' 1979 schedule. Those teams also accounted for every single Super Bowl champion for the past eight seasons. Pittsburgh had won 3; Dallas and Miami had won 2 each; and Oakland, 1.

The Oilers rightfully counted themselves among those teams with a real shot, but many obstacles stood in their way.

Only four teams on their schedule finished under .500 in 1978. Plus, they had to play division rival Pittsburgh twice.

Houston faced the Washington Redskins on the road in Week 1. Washington, coached by future Oiler head coach Jack Pardee, looked to build upon their previous year's 8-8 record.

Washington's biggest problem hailed from Tyler, Texas. Stopping Earl Campbell was a puzzle NFL defenses had yet to solve. Washington planned to line up strong safety Ken Houston where a linebacker sometimes played, to key in on Campbell.

Dan Pastorini wore a flak jacket and shoulder brace. He didn't practice that week, but he certainly showed up to play. "There's a switch," he said. "It goes off when you get out there and it's all on the line."

The switch went off and the Oilers kicked off their 1979 season.

Oiler kicker Toni Fritsch, a former pro soccer player from Austria, kicked two early field goals to put Houston ahead 6-0. So far, so good.

The second quarter, however, turned ugly for the Oilers. A special teams gaffe allowed a 52-yard punt return and led to a Mark Mosely field goal for Washington.

On the ensuing possession, Washington's defense intercepted Pastorini. Quarterback Joe Theismann hit tight end Jean Fugett for a touchdown, and the home team led, 10-6.

As if hitting the rewind button, Pastorini threw another interception. Washington scored another touchdown.

By halftime, a special teams mistake and two Pastorini interceptions donated 17 points worth of opening day gifts to the Redskins. The Oilers trailed 17-6 at halftime.

Owning the short end of the scoreboard at halftime wasn't new to the Oilers. They totaled 10 wins in 1978 and trailed at halftime in 5 of those wins. Twice they rallied from at least 10 points down. Both of those occasions had been on the road.

Houston needed a spark in the second half. They found it offensively.

Campbell started the second half's opening drive with 2 runs totaling 21 yards. Pastorini regrouped and found trusty Ken Burrough for 35 yards.

Then Earl did what only he could do.

Campbell followed center Carl Mauck and broke away from defensive tackle Dave Butz. He busted through a linebacker and met safety Mark Murphy head on. Campbell spun past Murphy and caused safety Tony Peters to grab nothing but air. Earl exploded downfield, outran diving linebacker Rich Milot, and fell backward into the end zone.

Five busted tackles. Thirteen yards. Six points.

Who else could run like that? Earl Campbell had to be seen to be believed. He broke through a defensive tackle and a linebacker. Spinning through the defense, he caused two other players to miss. Then, he quickly rebuilt speed to outrun another tackler. Back-to-back-to-back, all in a matter of seconds.

Washington responded with a touchdown drive of their own, and another Pastorini interception set up another Mark Mosely field goal.

Houston trailed by two touchdowns, 27-13, on the road, in the fourth quarter.

Houston decided to run directly at Washington's defensive strategy and sent running back Tim Wilson to block ahead of Campbell. The plan worked. The Oilers drove down to Washington's 14-yard line.

Billy Johnson then put on his playmaking shoes. Pastorini pitched him an easy touchdown, alone in the end zone, wide open. Billy busted into his trademark touchdown dance and the Oilers thought they had pulled to within seven points.

Those thoughts ended with a thud. Or maybe a clang. The extra point attempt bounced off an upright and failed.

The NFL wouldn't adopt the two-point conversion for another fifteen years. The Oilers still needed two scores to win.

The defense answered, and kicker Toni Fritsch redeemed himself. A defensive stop followed by a field goal pulled the Oilers to within 5 points. Could the defense get another stop? If so, would the Oilers have time enough to score?

Theismann handed off to future Hall of Fame running back John Riggins on first down. A bone-crushing hit followed. Then, a fumble. Then, an Oiler recovery. Houston had a first down on Washington's 29 with about six-and-a-half minutes left.

The Oilers needed a touchdown to win but didn't want to give Theismann enough time to win at home with long-range kicker Mark Mosely on his side.

Houston inched down the field, milking the clock. The offense faced a fourth-and-1, from the 8-yard line, with just over two minutes left.

Who else but Earl Campbell, right?

Right. Except that he slipped at the start of the play.

Washington's defense charged. The Oiler line maintained their ground. Campbell quickly regained stride and Pastorini handed him the ball. The Tyler Rose picked up the first down.

Next came the two-minute warning. On the next play, Campbell coasted across the goal line, ball firmly in hand. Toni Fritsch's extra point made it 29-27, Oilers.

The game ended with a Mark Mosely field goal attempt from 70 yards away. Not even the strong-legged Mosely came close to making that longshot.

The Oilers won the first game of the season as a team. Billy "White Shoes" Johnson proved he was back and ready to make big things happen alongside Ken Burrough. Double-O himself had a big catch. The defense forced a late fumble to overcome a missed extra point. Toni Fritsch kicked three field goals, and Earl Campbell played like Earl Campbell – 166 yards and 2 touchdowns.

Most importantly, the team didn't quit when they trailed by 11 points at halftime and by 14 in the fourth quarter. They didn't quit when the missed extra point made it more difficult to come back late in the game. Pastorini didn't quit despite throwing 3 interceptions while battling injuries. Campbell didn't quit after slipping on the fourth-down play. He instead called it his best slip ever. Robert Brazile certainly didn't quit. All week, NFL highlight reels showed him rolling over two offensive linemen to sack Joe Theismann.

The Oilers weren't like a balloon, deflating when things turned coldly against them. If anything, they were more like a pressurized chamber, gaining strength in situations where teams folded.

After the game, Leon Gray said he knew this team wouldn't quit. He experienced it on the other side as a member of the Patriots in 1978. Gray refused to quit against Washington with that game in mind.

The week was tight for the AFC Central Division as a whole. Both the Steelers and Browns needed overtime to win. Cincinnati, however, didn't score in their debut. The Oilers' 2-point squeaker put them in a three-way tie for first place. In the win column it looked as good as a 50-0 victory.

Next stop, Pittsburgh.

CHAPTER 4
Week 2 – AT PITTSBURGH

The Oilers and Steelers played their previous matchup under some of the ugliest weather conditions in AFC Championship Game history. Ice and slush coated the field at Three Rivers Stadium. On one famous play, Pittsburgh quarterback Terry Bradshaw slid a full 10 yards on his backside across the slick artificial turf.

The weather also affected ball security. The ball squirted about the place and the teams combined for 14 turnovers. That's right, 14 turnovers in a championship game – 9 by Houston.

Although the Oilers didn't look for excuses after the 34-5 thumping, fans and sportswriters who expected a close game pointed to the weather. Many wondered how the Oilers would fare under better conditions. They would find out in Week 2 of the 1979 season. The teams played under clear September skies, with temperatures in the mid-50s. Beautiful football weather.

Pittsburgh won the field position battle early. A short punt after Houston's second possession put the Steelers at midfield. Things got jumpy after that.

The Oilers knew Terry Bradshaw well. The defense expected his common snap count. Bradshaw introduced a longer one and the Oilers jumped offside. He tried it again. Another offsides. Bradshaw used the longer count a third time and gained another 5 yards via penalty. The officials flagged the Oilers for being offsides four times on the short drive that ended with Steeler running back Sidney Thornton crossing the goal line.

A 7-0 first-quarter deficit on the road isn't anything to get nervous about. The Oilers offense went to work, although the possession mimicked one under the conditions in the 1978 AFC Championship Game.

On first down, the Steelers sacked Pastorini and forced a fumble. Fortunately, Oiler center Carl Mauck recovered. Crisis avoided.

Until second down. Pastorini handed off to Tim Wilson who promptly coughed up the ball. Thankfully, he was able to recover it. Two fumbles back-to-back. Kind of strange, huh?

After two fumbles, the Oilers faced a third down on their own 8-yard line. Pastorini dumped a short pass to Earl Campbell. Earl made a nice catch, turned downfield…and fumbled. The ball bounced harmlessly out of bounds, short of the first down. Three plays, three fumbles. Luckily, no serious damage.

Oiler linebacker Robert Brazile didn't enjoy watching the Oilers fumble. He preferred Steeler fumbles. After another short punt gave Pittsburgh the ball on the Houston 43, field position that usually gave the Steelers easy pickings at home, Brazile crashed through the Steeler offensive line on first down. He popped Terry Bradshaw hard and forced a fumble. Steelers center Mike Webster recovered, but Brazile's disruptive play stifled the Steelers, who ended up punting as the first quarter expired.

Early in the second quarter, Pastorini hit Billy Johnson in stride for 25 yards to the Oiler 40. Both the Oiler drive and Billy's season were off to outstanding starts.

Pastorini drifted back to throw again, throwing on target, but the pass bounced off a receiver's hands and into the arms of Steeler linebacker Jack Lambert.

Houston's defense held the Steelers to a field goal. Pittsburgh led, 10-0.

The Oiler defense had played well thus far. The offense, however, struggled. Despite Steeler defensive line star L.C. Greenwood missing the game due to injury, the Steel Curtain defense held strong.

A backup named Tom Beasley stopped Campbell cold on a third-and-short to force another punt. It was that kind of day offensively. Fumbles, dropped passes, and backups stopping Campbell.

The Oilers finally got a break on defense. Linebacker Art Stringer intercepted Bradshaw. Houston now had a chance to gain momentum with about three minutes left in the half.

A sack, a dropped pass, and a third-down stop put that dream to rest quickly.

There would be one more glimmer of hope before halftime. Safety Mike Reinfeldt picked off another Bradshaw pass after Andy Dorris rushed the throw. Reinfeldt returned the ball to the Steeler 36-yard line with five seconds left in the first half.

Houston considered a 53-yard field goal attempt, but that seemed out of Toni Fritsch's range. Bum Phillips arched his bow and aimed for a touchdown. Houston flooded the right side of the field with Kenny Burrough, Billy Johnson, and Tim Wilson.

The line provided Pastorini plenty of protection. He lofted a pass into the end zone. Several players jumped for the ball, as if going for a rebound in basketball. Burrough reached higher than everyone and got his hands on it.

Jack Lambert and rookie defensive back Dwayne Woodruff hit Burrough before he came down with the catch, however, and the Oiler opportunity bounced away after impact. The Oilers were that close to being within 3 points at halftime.

Football is a funny game. Had Burrough scored, the Oilers would have taken momentum into the locker room, trailing on the road by only 3 points in a game they stalled offensively. Campbell only had 23 yards rushing. Pastorini netted only 16 yards passing. An Oiler touchdown at the end of the half would have changed the complexion of the game.

Houston's defense carried their tough play into the second half. Pittsburgh started with nice field position on their own 34, but Brazile and Dorris sacked Bradshaw. Reinfeldt then broke up a pass to John Stallworth.

The Steelers punted on fourth-and-long. Billy Johnson returned the kick. That surprised those who read that Bum Phillips reportedly said that Johnson was too valuable to return kicks.

At that point, early in the third quarter, the Steelers led, 10-0. Houston overcame a larger deficit on the road in Week 1.

On the Oilers' opening drive of the second half, Earl Campbell picked up a third-and-short, but a holding penalty erased the success.

When the teams replayed third down, Pittsburgh sacked Pastorini at the Oiler 4. Pastorini slowly got to his feet.

The Oilers punted. The Steelers started at their own 45 and quickly got into the end zone. Pittsburgh now led, 17-0.

Pastorini followed with an interception and the game looked like a rout similar to the 1978 AFC Championship Game. Houston's defense, however, forced a missed field goal.

Could that spark a turnaround for the Oilers? Another play or two like in the Washington game could get the Oilers back into the game with plenty of time left in the third quarter.

Instead, things only got worse. Way worse.

A penalty created a second-down-and-20, deep in Oiler territory. Pastorini looked to throw but faced heavy pressure. Linebacker Loren Toews knocked Pastorini's arm as he threw, and the ball jetted high into the air. Defensive lineman John Banaszak intercepted the deflected pass and rushed toward the goal line.

Only one Oiler stood in Banaszak's way – Dan Pastorini. Pastorini stopped the return but a crushing blow from Banaszak left Pastorini writhing in pain on the Three Rivers turf. Medical staff carried him off on a stretcher.

The Steelers scored a touchdown on the next play and led, 24-0.

Later in the third quarter, Billy "White Shoes" Johnson fielded a punt. An Oiler teammate crashed into him near the Pittsburgh sidelines. Steeler players quickly waved medical staff over. Trainers then carted Johnson off the field.

The slide continued on the scoreboard. Pittsburgh built a 38-0 lead before quarterback Gifford Nielsen avoided a shutout with a 5-yard touchdown pass to Guido Merkens in the final seconds.

After the game, Steeler linebacker Jack Lambert told papers that the Steelers played many great defensive games over the years, but this was one of their best. Pittsburgh held Campbell to 38 yards, his lowest total as a pro. They limited Houston's passing game to under 60 yards, notched 5 interceptions, and pounded Oiler quarterbacks for 5 sacks.

The weather was pleasant that afternoon, but the scoreboard's ugly result bore chilly resemblance to the 1978 AFC Championship Game.

Pastorini left the stadium with his arm in a sling. Johnson left on crutches.

The team returned home, one game behind both Pittsburgh and Cleveland in the AFC Central Division standings.

CHAPTER 5

Week 3 – HOME VS. KANSAS CITY

The Astrodome was *the* place to be on Sunday afternoons when the Oilers were in town. Fans created an atmosphere that was one-part hysteria, one-part pom-poms, and danced to fight songs. The scene blended a passion similar to college football with the exuberance of a rock concert filled with classic hits.

While the Oiler defense provided plenty of hits on the field, the Oiler offense produced two hits on the radio. Carl Mauck produced the first hit, called, "The Oiler Cannonball." The song mimicked Roy Acuff's country classic, "The Wabash Cannonball," with Oiler-flavored lyrics.

Mauck grew up listening to his father playing harmonica. One of Carl's grandfather's favorite songs was, "The Wabash Cannonball."

Mauck wrote, "The Oiler Cannonball," inspired by Earl Campbell's great rookie year and the Oilers' rise in 1978. After Mauck sang it to a sportswriter, one thing led to another, and the song was recorded at country star Mickey Gilley's studio. The record sold thousands of copies, and Mauck donated his profits to charity.

Ken Burrough followed that hit up with his disco jam, "The Super Bowl Itch." Ken's wife suggested to the local songwriters who wrote the song that Burrough record it. Double-0 proved a great fit and he wound up performing the song for a nationwide audience on Dinah Shore's show. Ken also donated his part of the proceeds to charity.

The city gave the Oilers so much. The team wanted to give back both in the community and in the win column.

The Oilers first home game of 1979 came in Week 3 against the Kansas City Chiefs.

Houston's injury report listed Billy Johnson as out. He learned that he tore all four knee ligaments at Pittsburgh. He asked the doctor if he could ever play football again. The doctor responded, "We'll see how you rehab."

Houston's injury report also listed Pastorini as out. That gave Gifford Nielsen his first opportunity to start a regular season game. Kansas City rookie Steve Fuller also gained his first pro start at quarterback.

Members of the 1960 Houston Oilers gathered at the game as part of a 20th-anniversary reunion. The Oilers won the American Football League championship in 1960 and 1961. George Blanda quarterbacked Houston to both championships. He said the Oilers challenged the NFL champion Philadelphia Eagles to a match in 1960, but never heard back.

The 1979 Oilers needed to overcome Pastorini's and Johnson's injuries to beat the Chiefs in Week 3 and to stay close with Pittsburgh and Cleveland in the division standings. Unfortunately, the Oilers injured list grew larger when Elvin Bethea pulled a muscle during pre-game warmups. The Oilers were now without two offensive starters and one on defense.

Houston's luck changed after kickoff. Linebacker Gregg Bingham recovered a Kansas City fumble, and Gifford Nielsen hit Mike Barber for 37 yards. Earl Campbell followed with a touchdown; the first rushing touchdown given up by the Chiefs in 1979.

The Oilers led, 7-0.

Kansas City's J.J. Smith later appeared to tie the game with a 55-yard punt return for a touchdown until Oiler defensive back Vernon Perry blocked the extra point.

The Oilers kept the lead and the Oiler fans kept cheering.

The cheering got louder when Tim Wilson raced into the end zone with a 24-yard screen pass. His score made it 14-6.

Earl Campbell was key to the play's success even though he didn't touch the ball. His fake duped the defense into running the opposite direction and opened things up for Wilson and his blockers.

Toni Fritsch later added two field goals and the Oilers won their home opener, 20-6.

Like the game at Washington, the Oilers won as a team. The defense basically shut out the Chiefs, as the visitor's only points came on a punt return. Mike Reinfeldt and J.C. Wilson snared 2 interceptions each, and Jesse Baker tallied his first NFL sack. The offensive line didn't allow a single sack and created enough running room for Campbell to gain over 100 yards. Gifford Neilsen played an excellent game as Pastorini heartily cheered him on.

Reporters noted Nielsen's fine performance and asked Bum Phillips if Nielsen had won the starting quarterback job. They pointed to Pastorini's injury and Dan's 6 interceptions over the first 2 games. Bum Phillips made clear that Pastorini was the team's starting quarterback. Offensive assistant King Hill confirmed that decision. Nielsen followed suit, in true team fashion.

The victory over Kansas City proved important, as both Pittsburgh and Cleveland knocked off their opponents. A loss would have placed Houston 2 games behind both teams in the AFC Central Division race. Instead, they remained only 1 game back.

CHAPTER 6
Week 4 – AT CINCINNATI

The Cincinnati Bengals stared with an 0-3 record, 3 games behind Pittsburgh and Cleveland. The Bengals' season, one that some predicted would be a winning season, already stood on the brink of disaster. The team desperately needed a win.

Desperate teams sometimes find desperate ways to win. Especially against divisional rivals. In this case, the Bengals owned the Oilers at Cincinnati's Riverfront Stadium, winning 7 of the last 9 on their turf.

One factor seemed to point in Houston's favor, however. Oiler quarterback Dan Pastorini suited up to play, while Cincinnati's franchise quarterback Ken Anderson sat out with an injury. The Oilers faced their second rookie quarterback in as many weeks.

This week's quarterback was Jack Thompson. Thompson set the NCAA career passing yards record at Washington State. The Bengals drafted him with the third-overall pick in the 1979 NFL Draft, before the Giants selected Phil Simms seventh overall and

San Francisco took a chance on a guy named Joe Montana at the end of the third round.

Going into Week 4, the Bengal defense had zero interceptions. Cincinnati's offense had yet to score a first-quarter touchdown. The Oilers quickly turned those stats into old news.

Pastorini served up Cincinnati's first interception of the year. Cincinnati's offense capitalized to score their first first-quarter touchdown of 1979. The score put Cincinnati up, 7-0.

The Bengals started their second possession from their own 45. Jack Thompson floated a beautiful pass to Billy Brooks for a long gain. It looked like a sure touchdown, but Brooks collapsed on his way to the end zone at the Oiler 19.

Brooks was next seen in street clothes and on crutches while watching the game from the sidelines.

The Bengals didn't let his play go for naught, however, and soon scored their second touchdown of the game. The Oilers trailed by 14.

The margin got wider as Houston's offense struggled. Pastorini threw his eighth interception of the season.

Although sacks by Ted Washington and Jesse Baker forced a punt, Houston soon gave the ball right back to Cincinnati with great field position.

Thompson engineered a 43-yard drive into the Oiler end zone. The Bengals led, 21-0. At this point in time, Jack Thompson's career greatly outshined those of his rookie counterparts, Joe Montana and Phil Simms.

Could things get any worse for the Oilers? Yes.

Rich Ellender, recently re-signed after being cut, fumbled the kickoff. The Bengals recovered. Andy Dorris tagged Thompson with a sack almost out of field goal range, but Cincinnati kicker Chris Bahr nailed a 52-yard attempt.

The Bengals led, 24-0.

Most teams closed shop when down by 24 points, but the Houston Oilers weren't like most teams. The Oilers beat New England after trailing 23-0 in 1978. What's one point more, one year later?

Ellender redeemed himself by returning the next kickoff to the 33-yard line. Earl Campbell picked up 15 yards to the Oiler 48. Mike Barber's catch put the Oilers at the Bengal 35. On third-and-11, Pastorini threw a dart into double coverage, this time to where only Kenny Burrough could catch it. Touchdown, Oilers.

The catch was Ken's 346th of his career, good enough for seventh on the NFL's all-time list at the time.

The Oiler defense stopped the Bengals cold on the ensuing possession. After the punt, Houston started on their own 46.

Pastorini threw two straight completions, one to Tim Wilson and the next to Rob Carpenter. He then ran a quarterback draw to the Bengal 28 and took a vicious hit.

Pastorini appeared woozy and lined up under guard instead of center for the next play. He then threw three straight incompletions.

The drive still led to points. Toni Fritsch kicked a 43-yard field goal to make it 24-10 at halftime.

Bum Phillips had a philosophy. Well, he had many philosophies. One particular philosophy proved right in this game.

"He coached big time that the first five minutes of the first and third quarter sets the pace and momentum for that half," tight end Mike Barber said.

Who would set the pace in the second half?

Former Bengal Boobie Clark signed with the Oilers after Cincinnati placed him on waivers during the preseason. Clark returned the favor by forcing a fumble on the opening kickoff of the second half. Houston recovered.

Pastorini hit Barber on a screen for 20 yards. Campbell rushed twice, the second time into the end zone. All of a sudden, it was 24-17.

The Oiler defense wanted their say. Robert Brazile sacked Jack Thompson to force a punt.

The second half pace had been set in Houston's direction. Houston's offense, defense, and special teams each contributed plays in the first five minutes of the second half.

Houston's offense sustained the momentum. Campbell picked up an Oiler first down. Barber picked up another. Pastorini then found Rich Caster for a 22-yard touchdown to tie the game at 24.

"It was a down and out route that I caught on the out portion of it," Caster remembered. "Cincinnati had blown the coverage somehow, and I was wide open. It was just a matter of turning and running 10 or 15 yards into the end zone. That was kind of one of those touchdowns that you never forget, one that made a big difference in the outcome of the game."

The Oilers weren't finished with their third-quarter explosion. Jesse Baker notched his third sack of the game. Tim Wilson's run on the Oilers next possession set up a Toni Fritsch field goal to put the Oilers ahead, 27-24.

The Oilers, the team that wouldn't quit, rallied from 24 points down to lead by 3.

Jack Thompson wouldn't quit either. He drove the Bengals into Houston territory in the fourth quarter. He called for a big play on third-and-1, a flea-flicker.

Thompson handed off to a running back. Instead of running, however, the back tossed the ball back to Thompson. Usually, linebackers and defensive backs bite on the play, and a downfield receiver is left wide open.

Oiler linebacker Gregg Bingham wasn't buying. He read the play when the running back grabbed the ball by its laces. He knew it was a pass. He sprinted downfield, his back to the action.

Bingham saw the intended receiver look up with his eyes, and knew the ball was coming his way. Bingham looked back and snatched the ball out of the air for an interception.

The Bengals wound up with one last shot, a 55-yard field goal attempt by Chris Bahr. Bahr, the Bengals second-round draft choice in 1976, fulfilled his promise and made it.

The 55-yard field goal energized the crowd into its loudest roar of the day. The kick also set a record for the longest field goal in team history. It stood alone as the Bengal record for over 30 years, and (as of 2020) remains tied as the longest in franchise history.

The Oilers held the ball at midfield as time ran out. An odd mix of a dropped pass, a sack, and Leon Gray losing his shoe cost Houston a chance to win the game in regulation.

Would the 24-point rally be for naught or would the Oilers prevail? Overtime held the story.

The two teams traded punts in overtime.

It looked like Houston forced another punt after Curley Culp's sack created a third-and-15. Two straight Thompson completions, however, put the Bengals within field goal range.

Bahr lined up for a 32-yard game-winning field goal -- and missed.

One might wonder how a kicker who just set a franchise record with a 55 yarder could miss from 32.

Gregg Bingham said it wasn't a choke on Bahr's part. He said Vernon Perry burst through the line to block the field goal. To avoid the block, Bahr pushed it a little too far to one side and missed. Like a pass rush hurries a quarterback into an incomplete pass, pressure can also force missed field goals.

The Bengals' defense responded and forced yet another Oiler punt. On the plus side, Houston downed the punt at the Cincinnati 5. The sequence completely flipped field position in Houston's favor.

After a solid defensive stand, Houston got the ball back at the Cincinnati 41 with very little time left. It appeared that the worst the Oilers could do was tie. Though not as bad as a loss, a tie would likely place Houston further behind Pittsburgh and Cleveland in the divisional race.

On Houston's third-down play, Rob Carpenter appeared to make the first down. Referee Jim Tunney, however, spotted the ball further back. Video replay showed Carpenter likely made the first down, but in 1979 Bum Phillips didn't have any recourse to challenge the spot.

He did, however, have Earl Campbell. Even though everybody in Riverfront Stadium knew Campbell would get the ball, he outran defensive back Ken Riley all the way to the Bengal 18.

In just one play, Campbell turned a likely tie into a likely win. Especially with the sure-footed Toni Fritsch on board.

Then, the unthinkable. Earl Campbell fumbled on the next play. The Bengals recovered.

Second guessers scratched their heads wondering why Houston didn't just kick the field goal on first down.

Then, like a ray of sunshine, a bright yellow penalty flag lay on the field. Referee Jim Tunney this time gave hope to the Oilers. Cincinnati was offsides on the play, and the Oilers had a second chance.

Second guessers relaxed. Bum Phillips wasted no time in getting Toni Fritsch on the field. From 29 yards out, victory seemed as certain as making an extra point.

Until it wasn't that certain.

Fritsch's wavering kick bounced off the inside half of the upright.

Then, like a magic rainbow, it somehow found its way through the uprights and over the crossbar.

The Oilers won, 30-27. Teammates triumphantly carried Toni Fritsch off the field.

The field goal looked ugly on television. On the scoreboard and in the standings, however, it looked straight down the middle.

Pittsburgh and Cleveland both won to stay undefeated. The Riverfront Miracle kept the Oilers within striking distance of first place in the AFC Central. A date with Cleveland at the Astrodome marked next Sunday's plans. Houston could at least tie Cleveland by the end of September.

The 24-point rally set a franchise record. The Oilers previously set the record in 1978 with the 23-point comeback at New England. One point more, one year later.

Those two games still stand as the two biggest comeback wins in Oilers/Titans franchise history (as of 2020).

Just like at Washington in Week 1, the Oilers didn't quit. The defense bullied the Bengals for 7 sacks. Houston's special teams forced a fumble and a missed field goal attempt. Earl Campbell rushed for 158 yards and a touchdown. Pastorini recovered from two early interceptions and tossed two touchdowns.

Rich Caster talked about how a football team's character can overcome adversity and win after falling behind.

"We had a bunch of guys there who had shown that they were winners, proven veterans who knew what the game of football was all about. We knew if we kept pressing and pushing forward, then there was a good chance that things would turn around for us.

"If a team works hard enough and is given enough opportunities, and make all the right plays, with little exception they can turn any momentum around. It was working for us that day and that year."

Leon Gray told reporters that the Oilers didn't hit the panic button after falling behind. Bum Phillips added that the field goal at the end of the first half stood paramount, giving the coaches and players something positive to discuss at halftime.

Although Houston's comeback set the all-time club record, it simply tied for the NFL's best comeback of the day. The Denver Broncos trailed the Seattle Seahawks 34-10, but rallied to win at home. The 24-point comeback tied the Broncos' team record that still stands.

CHAPTER 7
Week 5 – HOME VS. CLEVELAND

In December of 1962, Houston Oiler Charley Tolar rushed 29 times against the New York Titans, now known as the New York Jets. The 29 rushing attempts in a single game set an Oiler team record.

Earl Campbell broke Tolar's record against Washington in Week 1 of the 1979 season by logging 32 attempts. Campbell tied his shiny new club record against Kansas City in Week 3. Against the Bengals, he broke his new record with 34 carries, enough to match his jersey number.

Campbell now had 114 rushing attempts on the year. New England's Sam Cunningham was second in the AFC with 70 attempts, 44 behind Earl.

Campbell was a special back on a team that produced a special comeback at Cincinnati. In practice that week, they had a special visitor. A long limousine pulled up to the team's facility and out stepped "The Champ," Muhammad Ali. He dropped by to say hello to the Oilers.

The undefeated Cleveland Browns dropped by to say hello that Sunday. The Browns had just clobbered the Cowboys on *Monday Night Football* the week before at Cleveland.

Although Cleveland celebrated the victory, the win proved costly. They lost two important players to knee sprains. Defensive end Lyle Alzado's injury occurred in bizarre fashion – a security guard fell on top of him while holding back excited fans after the win over Dallas. Both Alzado and running back Greg Pruitt would miss the Oiler game.

On Thursday, the injury bug bit Houston. Earl Campbell suffered a thigh bruise in practice. Earl was expected to suit up for the game.

The Browns replaced their 1,000-yard rusher Greg Pruitt with the talented Mike Pruitt. The two were not related but were both effective.

The crankshaft of the Browns lineup was star quarterback Brian Sipe, who would win the NFL's MVP award the next year. Sipe played college football at San Diego State under head coach Don Coryell, the offensive wizard who now coached the potent San Diego Chargers.

Sipe and the Browns won the coin toss and elected to receive, but then immediately lost yardage.

Ted Washington and Andy Dorris busted through the line to sack Sipe on the first offensive play of the game. The second play was even better for Houston. Elvin Bethea recovered a fumble.

Bethea spoke about the joy of making big plays early. "When the ball's on the ground everyone jumps on it and the first one there owns the ball. You always hope that you can get the ball to the offensive team as quick as possible so they can get on the board and we can have a wonderful day!"

The Oilers kicked a field goal to get on the scoreboard. Campbell added a touchdown and Houston led, 10-0, in front of a rocking Astrodome crowd that fed off the home team's momentum.

The Browns countered with a field goal and later drove to the Oiler 14. The game's outcome unfolded around a chain of events shortly thereafter.

Houston's defense forced a failed field goal attempt. The Oiler offense followed with an 80-yard touchdown drive highlighted by Mike Barber's 35-yard catch. Earl Campbell capped the drive with his second touchdown of the day.

Cleveland's season was off to its best start since 1963, but the Browns were off to a terrible start in the Astrodome that Sunday. Sipe hoped to reverse course with aggressive passing.

Oiler defensive coordinator Ed Biles told cornerback J.C. Wilson to take a chance on an interception. The gamble paid off. Wilson picked off Sipe and dashed 34 yards into the end zone, granting Houston a 24-3 second-quarter lead.

Biles explained that some receivers gave away their routes with their footwork. These tendencies revealed themselves during a game or on film. For example, a receiver might go to the outside every time he stuttered his steps. Sometimes the length of his stride gave additional information. A shorter stride might give away a short route, a longer stride might reveal a deeper route.

Defensive back Willie Alexander added that he sometimes counted steps to learn a receiver's tendencies. He learned that one opponent either cut by his sixth step or went long. Another slowed down on his third step every time he cut inside.

Alexander emphasized that the best receivers he faced, Hall of Famers like Charlie Joiner and Lynn Swann, wouldn't give such tells. Many other receivers, however, weren't as poker faced. Both he and Biles said the receivers likely didn't realize that they were giving themselves away.

You might remember that Bum Phillips emphasized the importance of first five minutes of the first and third quarters. Houston recovered a fumble in the first five minutes of the first half against the Browns and built a huge lead by the second quarter. The Oilers kept their foot on the gas coming out for the second half.

Pastorini likely earned extra credit with his coach on a 12-play, 66-yard drive that erased over seven minutes off the clock to start the second half. The forceful yet tactical drive thwarted the Browns second-half game plan to aggressively attack offensively to get back in the game. Cleveland never got the chance.

Houston bounced away with a decisive 31-10 victory.

The huge lead allowed Earl Campbell to rest his thigh bruise. He only carried the ball three times in the second half, although one resulted in his third touchdown of the game.

Pastorini's stat sheet sparkled with zero interceptions. The defense sacked opposing quarterback Brian Sipe five times and intercepted him twice.

Houston defeated a divisional rival with another team-based win, and the Oilers ended September with a 4-1 record.

The Oilers found a friend in the Philadelphia Eagles that day. The Eagles knocked off the Steelers in the City of Brotherly Love, bumping Houston, Cleveland, and Pittsburgh into a first-place tie.

The Oilers closed out September tied for first despite getting trounced by the Steelers and suffering numerous injuries. Houston rallied on the road for two wins in games they trailed by 14 points or more.

Since trailing Cincinnati 24-0, the Oilers outscored opponents 61-13.

The crisp air of October ushered in the challenge of sustaining that momentum.

PART 3
TWISTS AND TURNS ALONG KIRBY DRIVE

CHAPTER 8
Week 6 – HOME VS. ST. LOUIS

The St. Louis Cardinals, now known as the Arizona Cardinals, tumbled into the Astrodome with a dismal 1-4 record. Oiler fans relished the thought of an easy victory. The more knowledgeable fans doubled their excitement after reading that week's full NFL schedule.

Pittsburgh and Cleveland played each other that week. An Oiler win guaranteed that Houston would stay in a first-place tie with the winner. They would also move one game ahead of the loser.

Losing records can be deceiving in the National Football League. The 1-4 Cardinals lost by only one point to Dallas in Week 1. Pittsburgh needed 17 fourth-quarter points to narrowly defeat the songbirds.

Rookie sensation Ottis Anderson led the Cardinal running attack. Anderson climbed the NFL rushing leaderboard and challenged Walter Payton and Earl Campbell for tops in rushing yardage. The Oilers saw Anderson in their first preseason game, a 9-7 Oiler victory.

The Cardinals-Oilers regular season matchup also started as a low-scoring affair. Neither team scored in the first quarter, quieting a home crowd eager to erupt. The Cardinals then swallowed a chunk of game time with a 16-play touchdown drive to lead, 7-0.

The home crowd finally got a chance to roar late in the second quarter. Earl Campbell latched onto a 46-yard screen pass to set up a 4-yard touchdown run.

Only 22 seconds later, Pastorini and Burrough hit an 11-yard touchdown pass after Cardinal quarterback Jim Hart threw an interception. The Oilers held a 14-7 halftime edge.

Cardinal head coach Bud Wilkinson earned legendary status in the college ranks at Oklahoma. His Sooners won 47 consecutive games, which still stands as an NCAA record.

Wilkinson figured a good game of keep away could stop the Oiler offense. Jim Hart carried out the plan, and the Cardinals pecked away both yardage and game time to start the second half.

Houston finally got the ball after St. Louis kicked a field goal nine minutes into the third quarter. Houston's Toni Fritsch countered with a 51-yard field goal – the second longest of his career – early in the fourth quarter.

The Oilers led, 17-10.

The Oiler defense stood tough and forced a fourth-and-14. Cardinal punter Steve Little stood ready.

Little was the Cardinals' first-round draft choice in 1978. He was best known for kicking long field goals, but field goal kickers sometimes doubled as punters in the 1970s. It turned out that Steve Little played quarterback in high school and could also pass.

Little took the fourth-and-14 snap, faked the punt, and tossed to running back Theotis Brown for a first down. St. Louis soon scored a 1-yard touchdown, and the game was tied at 17.

The Oilers flirted with disaster the entire game. Missed assignments and missed blocks allowed St. Louis to pour gasoline on Houston's victory plans. A Pastorini interception with just over two minutes remaining provided a lit match.

The Cardinals followed up with a game-winning touchdown. The Oilers lost at home, 24-17.

Houston also lost playmaking linebacker Art Stringer for at least four weeks.

Meanwhile, Browns quarterback Brian Sipe threw for 351 yards and 5 touchdowns against the Steelers – and *lost*. Pittsburgh posted 51 points against Cleveland, powered by 361 yards rushing. Three Pittsburgh running backs – Franco Harris, Rocky Bleier, and Sidney Thornton, each rushed for at least 80 yards. The game, played in Cleveland, lofted Pittsburgh into sole possession of first place in the AFC Central.

Houston and Cleveland both slipped one game behind.

CHAPTER 9

Week 7 – AT BALTIMORE

The loss to St. Louis provided new talking points for Dan Pastorini's critics. Members of Houston's Touchdown Club tagged Bum Phillips with questions regarding the starting quarterback position.

Phillips responded by saying, "Dan Pastorini is my quarterback. Period."

Bum Phillips stuck with Pastorini despite the arm injury and lackluster stats. He defended Pastorini against critics.

Maybe it was because Pastorini had a high ceiling. His best was comparable to just about any other NFL quarterback. Maybe Bum rallied behind Pastorini because of Dan's experience and knowledge of the game. Maybe it was because Phillips didn't like the idea of the press or anyone else telling him how to coach.

It could have been any of those things, a combination of all of them, or none of them. Bum's only explanation was, "Period."

There were Oiler fans who loved Dan Pastorini, and those who hated him.

Two things about Pastorini that even his doubters couldn't question were his toughness and his loyalty. He lined up for every game he was physically capable of playing in and in every single one of those games, he gave everything he had. He never gave 50 percent, he never gave 80 percent, and he never quit, regardless of the score.

The starting quarterback's attitude affects the team's attitude. When players see their quarterback giving up, it's harder for them to believe they have a chance to win. When players see their quarterback play through pain and tell them that a 24-0 deficit is doable, it's harder to give up, especially after you win under those conditions.

Pastorini wasn't unlike a lot of players on the 1979 Oilers. They showed up. They didn't quit. They played hurt. They fed off each other's determination. They might not have gotten along every day during the week, but on Sunday they fought for each other, believed in each other, and refused to quit on one another.

More than anything, they refused to quit on Bum Phillips, and Bum Phillips darn sure wasn't going to quit on his any of his players. Period.

Like the St. Louis Cardinals, the Baltimore Colts entered their game against the Oilers with only one regular season victory. Also similar to the Cardinals, they played close games against good teams. They lost to Pittsburgh by four. They lost to undefeated Tampa Bay by three. The Browns needed overtime to defeat the Colts.

Baltimore's biggest loss of the season was quarterback Bert Jones in Week 1. Jones reinjured the shoulder that sidelined him for most of the 1978 season. He led the Colts to the playoffs for three straight seasons before the injury, but their playoff hopes faded without him in both '78 and '79.

Houston's pass rush provided an early spark on that clear, cool October Sunday in Baltimore. Linebacker Ted Washington forced a Colt fumble. Jesse Baker scooped it up and took it to the house. The 20-yard return gave the Oilers an early 7-0 lead.

The Colts returned the kickoff 58 yards, and veteran quarterback Greg Landry engineered a short touchdown drive. The Colts missed the extra point, however, and Houston held a 7-6 lead.

Houston punted and a series of events set the tone for the rest of the game. The Colts drove close enough for a go-ahead field goal attempt but missed.

The Oiler offense took charge and drove all the way to set up a fourth-and-1 on Baltimore's 7-yard line. Houston lined up for a field goal, but Phillips called time out. He pulled Toni Fritsch off the field.

Rather than go for three points, why not go to number 3-4, Mr. Earl Campbell?

Campbell didn't just pick up one yard for the first down – he picked up all seven yards for a touchdown.

Campbell was on the move again after halftime.

On the Oilers first possession, he scored on a 20-yard run to make it 21-6. Later in the third quarter, he picked up another first down on a fourth-and-1, this time from the Oilers' 38-yard line. That's how much confidence the team had in Earl Campbell. Campbell capped off the drive with a 2-yard touchdown, giving the Oilers a 28-9 lead in the third quarter.

His work for the afternoon was complete.

Both Campbell and Pastorini sat out most of the fourth quarter, and the Oilers won, 28-16. The game showcased the greatness of Earl Campbell, who racked up 149 yards and 3 touchdowns in three quarters worth of work.

The Tyler Rose now had 11 touchdowns in 9 games. The NFL's single-season record for rushing touchdowns stood at 19. Campbell needed to average a touchdown a game to break the record.

Pastorini's stats again looked awful on paper. Five completions for 49 yards. In the win column, however, those stats looked as good as a 300-yard day.

The win put the Oilers at 5-2 on the season. The Browns lost and slipped to 4-3, a game behind the Oilers in the AFC Central standings.

The Bengals earned their first win of the season, in a game nobody, not even their most ardent fans, thought they'd have a chance. The Bengals thrashed the Pittsburgh Steelers, 34-10.

Cincinnati's victory made San Francisco the only winless team in the NFL, but they and their rookie head coach Bill Walsh would soon find their way.

The Oilers had found their way into a first-place tie with Pittsburgh. Forget the recent loss to St. Louis. What a difference a week makes.

CHAPTER 10

Week 8 – AT SEATTLE

There is an old theory in sports: players tend to play better against teams that traded them away. The player enjoys proving the other team wrong. That theory found new evidence in the gridiron laboratory of Seattle's Kingdome during an experiment held on October 21, 1979.

The 5-2 Oilers lined up against the 2-5 Seahawks. One of Seattle's wins came against the winless San Francisco 49ers, so it may have come at a discount. Either way, the Oilers were favored to win this one.

The Seahawks were a fairly new team. In 1976, the NFL added two new expansion teams, Seattle and Tampa Bay. Nineteen seventy-nine was Seattle's fourth year in the league.

Nineteen seventy-nine also marked the fourth year of future Hall of Fame receiver Steve Largent's career. In 1976, the Houston Oilers drafted Largent in the fourth round. After four preseason games, the team handed him a bus ticket home to Oklahoma.

Largent played his college ball at Tulsa. His college coach Jerry Rhome worked for the Seahawks as an assistant in 1976. Rhome convinced the Seahawks to trade an eighth-round draft choice to Houston for Largent. The Oilers loved the idea since they were on their way to releasing him.

Houston later used the draft pick on another player that didn't make their roster. Steve Largent, however, ended up on the Seahawks' roster of all-time greats.

In the week leading up to the Oilers-Seahawks game, Earl Campbell suffered from the effects of his thigh bruise and missed a full week of practice.

In the game, the Seahawks scored first on a touchdown pass from quarterback Jim Zorn to running back Sherman Smith. Dan Pastorini countered with a touchdown pass to Mike Barber to tie the game at 7.

Steve Largent committed his first act of vengeance against the Oilers in the second quarter, pulling in a 45-yard touchdown pass to give the upstart Seahawks a 14-7 halftime lead.

Efren Herrera kicked two third-quarter field goals for Seattle and the Oilers trailed 20-7 going into the fourth quarter.

Two Houston touchdowns could still win the game. Could the Oilers pull off another fourth-quarter miracle like the one at Washington?

Maybe, if they still had Steve Largent on their team. Largent caught his second long touchdown of the game, this one for 55 yards, and the Seahawks led 27-7 early in the fourth quarter. The Seahawk defense added their own flavor to the Oilers' misery by returning a fumble 54 yards for a touchdown shortly thereafter.

Seattle walked away with a 34-14 home victory, giving them a 3-5 record.

The Oilers dropped to 5-3. Cleveland also reached 5-3 with a one-point win over the now pesky Bengals. A botched extra point made the difference in that game.

The Steelers kicked several successful extra points in their *Monday Night Football* 42-7 drubbing of the Denver Broncos.

The AFC Central's screenwriter once again typed up the familiar scene of Houston tied for second behind Pittsburgh.

The Seattle game was Houston's second loss in three weeks. Both losses were to teams that Houston expected to beat.

At 5-3, the Oilers were still very much alive in the NFL's playoff hunt. At that moment, however, the loss to Seattle looked particularly bad.

At season's end, the loss to Seattle wasn't as bad as it originally looked. After the Seahawks beat Houston, they later won 5 of 6 and eventually finished 9-7 on the season. They were a winning team disguised as also-rans before their tilt against the Oilers.

No word from Steve Largent on whether he really had revenge on his mind for the Oilers-Seahawks game. While it's easy to criticize the Oilers for trading Largent, they did already have established receivers Kenny Burrough and Billy "White Shoes" Johnson already on their roster in 1976.

Critics targeting Dan Pastorini grumbled louder after the loss to Seattle, despite the fact that his two touchdown passes accounted for all of Houston's scoring. One columnist wondered if he wasn't the quarterback he once was, with his best games already in the record books. Another observed that Pastorini couldn't make some of the same throws he made the previous season.

Reproach wasn't reserved for Pastorini alone. One writer asked how pro players could display a subpar performance when they only play 16 days out of the year. Another surmised that the 10 wins in

1978 were a fluke and tossed 1975's 10-4 record under Bum Phillips into the same category.

Other writers saw a bigger picture, noting that Earl Campbell had only three carries against Seattle because of the thigh bruise and Ted Washington missed the game with a broken hand.

A *Houston Chronicle* reporter asked Bum Phillips if he remembered a team with as many injuries as the Oilers.

Phillips answered that he had never seen so many injuries on a team still in the playoff hunt.

CHAPTER 11
Bum And His Crew

Bum Phillips was born in Orange, Texas in 1923. His family moved to Beaumont during the Great Depression. The nickname, "Bum" came from a sister who either couldn't pronounce the word, "brother" or used Bum as an abbreviation of, "bumble bee" after Phillips was stung as a young child. Those are the two versions that Phillips listed in his autobiography, *Bum Phillips: Coach, Cowboy, Christian.*

The connotations of the word, "bum" didn't bother Phillips. He said he didn't mind the name as long as somebody didn't say, "You're a bum!"

Phillips experienced a hardscrabble upbringing throughout his youth. He learned the value of hard work early during the Great Depression.

He played high school football, despite his father's objections, and helped his school win a regional championship during his senior year.

Bum joined the Marines in 1942, after a year at Lamar Junior College. He joined the 4th Marine Raiders, commanded by James

Roosevelt, the eldest son of President Franklin Roosevelt. Bum fought in the Pacific and his battalion suffered heavy casualties. He spent 18 months in combat. His war experiences and hardiness during the Great Depression affected the way he coached and lived for the rest of his life.

He returned home and re-entered Lamar Junior College. He played football on a G.I. Bill scholarship. He later transferred to Stephen F. Austin State University and earned a degree. He was then offered an assistant coaching position at Nederland High School in Nederland, Texas.

Phillips became Nederland's head coach the next season. He coached high school ball in Texas for many years, and spent one year as Bear Bryant's assistant at Texas A&M.

Bryant hoped Phillips would follow him to Alabama, but Phillips declined. Bum wanted to stay in Texas. He coached high school ball and spent one year as head coach at Texas Western, now known as UTEP. Later, he worked as defensive coordinator for the University of Houston.

While Phillips worked for the Cougars, Hall of Fame coach Sid Gillman piloted the San Diego Chargers, one of the top teams in the American Football League. Gillman wanted to hire a new defensive assistant and believed college coaches worked harder to develop players than most pro coaches.

Gillman placed calls to some of college football's top head coaches, including Darrell Royal of Texas and Frank Broyles of Arkansas. Gillman asked if they knew of anyone who would make a great defensive assistant for the Chargers. The name Bum Phillips kept coming up.

Gillman called Phillips and hired him over the phone.

A pro job was too good to turn down even if it meant leaving the Lone Star State. Phillips flew out to San Diego to join the team and was one of the last passengers to deboard the plane. One man stood at the gate when Phillips got off.

He approached Phillips and said, "You must be Bum Phillips."

Phillips answered, "You must be Sid Gillman."

That was the first time that they met each other in person.

Gillman resigned from the Chargers in the early 1970s. He also resigned for the entire coaching staff, including Bum Phillips. Phillips briefly worked at SMU and Oklahoma State until Gillman called again.

Oilers owner Bud Adams had hired Gillman to turn the Houston Oilers franchise around. Gillman hired Phillips as his defensive coordinator. After the Oilers endured back-to-back 1-13 seasons, they finished 7-7 in 1974, their first full year with Gillman as head coach.

Gillman won UPI's NFL Coach of the Year honors but stepped down as head coach. He remained general manager, but only for a brief period of time.

By the time the 1975 season started, Bum Phillips was both the head coach and general manager of the Houston Oilers.

The first trade Phillips made was to obtain center Carl Mauck from San Diego. Mauck and Phillips had bonded over beers on road trips when Phillips worked for the Chargers. Mauck's father fought in the Pacific Theater during World War 2, so he and Phillips found common ground to swap stories during flights.

When you speak to players, all describe Phillips as a players' coach. He respected the players and earned the players' respect. Phillips allowed them the latitude to be responsible for their own behavior and work ethic.

Andy Dorris put it this way: "After practice Bum would tell us, 'Look, you all are professionals. If you want to stay after practice and run sprints, you do that. If you want to stay after practice and lift weights, you do that. If you want to go home and get off your feet and get some rest, you do that as well.' He really gave us ownership of the team."

Bum also worked to cultivate a family atmosphere. He figured that a person would fight harder for a family member than for a friend. He would tell players to gather, but then told them to sit with a teammate they didn't know. That move bonded more and more players together.

The family included the whole coaching staff. Carl Mauck says Phillips brought coaches and players together for fun during training camp.

Phillips would occasionally have beer and pizza parties during the season and the players appreciated it. In fact, after the 1978 comeback against the Patriots, Phillips grabbed the plane's intercom on the flight home. He told the players to call their wives and girlfriends and let them know they weren't coming home. Instead, they were all going out with Bum to celebrate.

That doesn't mean Phillips didn't believe in hard work. Quite the opposite. Mauck says one of Phillips' favorite sayings was, "Hard work and good times go together, but the hard work comes first."

Phillips knew when to work hard and when the players needed a break. Elvin Bethea says that one thing that made Phillips great is he knew what buttons to push for each individual player and when to push those buttons. He also gauged the team as a whole and cut practices short if necessary.

Phillips believed that if players practiced too hard, then they wouldn't have much left on Sunday. Moreover, he told players to save their best hitting for opponents rather than teammates. Robert Brazile remembers Bum scolding him and Earl Campbell during a rough practice.

"One day me and Earl was getting a little tough (with each other). Bum said, 'Guys, let me tell you: the Houston Oilers are not on our schedule. We play Pittsburgh, Cleveland, Cincinnati, and the other teams in the NFL. The Houston Oilers are not on our schedule. We're not going to beat up on each other! We're not going to be tackling each other, Robert!'"

Bum Phillips lived on a ranch. He raised cattle. In a day when NFL coaches mostly wore suits on the sidelines, Phillips wore a cowboy hat and boots. Well, sometimes a cowboy hat. His mother taught him never to wear a hat indoors, so he left the hat at home for games inside the Astrodome.

Colorful characters powered the NFL's popularity in the 1970s. Bum Phillips fit perfectly into the cast, especially after the "Urban Cowboy" fad caught on.

Phil Tuckett briefly played with the San Diego Chargers while Bum was an assistant. Tuckett later worked for NFL Films. As a result, NFL Films produced many segments featuring Bum Phillips. One showed the Oilers playing cards together, another covered Bum at his ranch. One followed Bum to Juarez, Mexico to have custom boots made. Naturally, Phillips and Tuckett became lifelong friends.

Tuckett says Bum also built a community atmosphere outside of football. On weeks when NFL Films sent Tuckett to Houston for Oiler games, he attended breakfasts that Phillips organized. The breakfasts wouldn't have anything to do about football and included Phillips' friends from his high school coaching days and country music singers. Tuckett remembers Bum pointing one particular individual out to him.

"You see that guy?" Phillips said. "That guy's so tough it took John Wayne to play him in a movie."

The man was firefighter Red Adair.

Tuckett also remembers being at the airport with Phillips. Airport personnel wanted to seat Phillips in a special spot for his flight and asked him to come to where the passengers unloaded.

Tuckett figured that Phillips would be mobbed by fans as they got off the plane.

Instead, people merely said, "Hi, Coach," and shook his hand. While some coaches left fans starstruck and begging for autographs, Phillips' personality didn't need that. He had a different relationship with Oiler fans. He didn't need to be treated like a celebrity. Fans respected and appreciated him for that.

Phillips hired an exceptional coaching staff. He promoted Ed Biles from assistant to defensive coordinator when he took the reins in 1975. Biles played college football at Miami of Ohio under Ara Parseghian and previously worked for the New Orleans Saints and New York Jets.

While Sid Gillman was head coach, the Oilers started using a 3-4 defensive scheme with three defensive linemen and four linebackers. Phillips and Biles modeled Houston's defense after the Miami Dolphins' defense that won Super Bowls 7 and 8. The Dolphins were the first NFL team to use the 3-4. Miami called it the 5-3, after linebacker Bob Mathias, who sported the number 53 on his jersey.

Phillips and Biles watched tons of Dolphins game film. They told Gillman that they needed a premier nose guard to make the defense work.

Gillman pulled off one of the slyest trades in Houston history, trading John Matuszak to the Kansas City Chiefs for Curley Culp and a first-round draft choice. The Oilers drafted linebacker Robert Brazile with that pick. Two Hall of Famers in one shot.

Culp said that Biles and the rest of the coaching staff did a great job in breaking down film and reading opposing teams' formations.

Biles was big on watching game film and had a knack for reading tendencies of teams and players. He explains what he noticed about Steelers Hall of Fame quarterback Terry Bradshaw.

"Terry, whenever he would back straight out, he was going to throw the ball to his left or to the middle. If he turned coming out, coming out sideways so to speak, he was going to throw the ball to the right side or to the middle.

"So, your free safety could get a great jump. Unfortunately, they had Swann and Stallworth who were two great receivers. Sometimes you'd have them double covered and they'd go up and take the ball away from you.

"But that's the kind of defensive coaching that you do in the NFL trying to give your team the opportunity to take advantage of a so-called 'tell'."

Bum Phillips once mentioned to Biles that he was thinking of hiring his son Wade as an assistant. Biles encouraged him to do so.

Wade Phillips was the defensive line coach for the 1979 Oilers. He still worked in the NFL as late as 2019, as the Los Angeles Rams defensive coordinator. Wade dressed up like his father to honor Bum before the Rams matchup against New England in Super Bowl 53. Wade Phillips has also served as head coach of the Buffalo Bills, Dallas Cowboys, and Denver Broncos, as well as other teams on an interim basis.

Before joining the Oilers, he worked in the college ranks on the staffs at Oklahoma State and Kansas. Phillips also played linebacker at the University of Houston.

Offensive assistant King Hill was an All-American quarterback at Rice and led the Owls to the 1958 Cotton Bowl. He was the first-overall draft pick in the 1958 NFL Draft and played over ten seasons, mostly for the Cardinals and Eagles.

The Oilers' media guide referred to Hill as the "Dean of Oiler coaches."

Dan Pastroini called King Hill one of the most intelligent football minds he ever worked with. Pastorini said Hill simplified the

Oilers' play numbering system into a quick, easy to understand format. For example, the 500 series of plays would be a play-action pass. One of the running plays was called a 36 run.

The system allowed Pastorini to quickly change play calls at the line of scrimmage and gave him enormous flexibility. Pastorini owned the opportunity to survey defensive formations and make pre-snap adjustments.

If he called 536 in the huddle and saw that the play action didn't match up well against the defense's formation, he could immediately change it to a 76 – a drop drawback pass. The wide receiver would know to run a curl pattern, the halfback knew to run to the flat, and the lineman knew their blocking assignments.

Pastorini explains: "It allowed me to spend time at the line of scrimmage because now I can see how the defensive linemen are lined up. I can see the angles our linemen can make. I would audible to a run or pass – whatever I wanted to run. A lot of times I'd get in the huddle and just say, 'Check with me.'

"I would walk up to the line of scrimmage. Whatever number I called first, two, three, or four, that was the go count. The next three numbers were the play. I'd call it out, '536! 536!' and let it sink in for a second. And I'd say, "Hut! Hut!" and then go."

Pastorini says that King Hill's offensive architecture framed Houston's most productive years on offense.

Bill Walsh inspired many of Hill's ideas. The Oilers saw Walsh's offensive designs twice a year when Walsh worked as Cincinnati's offensive coordinator. Hill took notes.

Oiler offensive line coach Joe Bugel took over the job in 1976. In 1978, Houston gave up the fewest sacks in the NFL.

Bugel worked for the Detroit Lions before coming to Houston. He later became one of the most successful offensive line coaches in NFL history while working under Joe Gibbs in Washington. He created an offensive line affectionately known as the "Hogs" during some of the franchise's most glorified seasons.

The Oiler staff also included former LSU star Andy Bourgeois coaching the offensive backfield and former Broncos assistant Bob Gambold coaching the defensive backfield. John Paul Young coached special teams.

Bum Phillips and his staff worked hard to help players achieve their maximum potential. Mike Barber said Phillips once told him that if he couldn't help bring out Barber's talent as a player, then he failed as a coach. Later, Hall of Fame quarterback Fran Tarkenton called Barber one of the best tight ends in the NFL during a nationally televised game.

At the midway point of the 1979 season, the Oilers owned a 5-3 record. Bum Phillips and his staff needed to dig deep and bring out the best in each player to achieve this team's potential and the dream of reaching Super Bowl 14.

PART 4
DIGGING DEEPER

CHAPTER 12

Week 9 – HOME VS. NEW YORK JETS

Week 9 kicked off the second half of the season. Playoff positioning bolstered the importance of the games. Teams around the .500 mark neared cliffs of trouble, in danger of plummeting downward.

The New York Jets and Houston Oilers were two such teams. The Jets were 4-4 coming in, having won two straight games.

The Oilers stood at 5-3. They had lost two of three and faced a brutal schedule moving forward. Both reigning conference champions, Pittsburgh and Dallas, loomed on the horizon. So did recent Super Bowl winners Oakland and Miami. Only one team on Houston's remaining schedule stood without a solid chance of making the playoffs.

That made Week 9 against the Jets sort of an early playoff game. The Jets could fall completely off the playoff cliff with a loss. A loss for Houston might mean dropping at least one game back of both Pittsburgh and Cleveland in the AFC Central.

Earl Campbell still ached from the thigh bruise suffered over three weeks ago. Elvin Bethea still nursed a sore knee. Ted Washington and second-round draft choice Mike Stensrud were both out. The NFL didn't have bye weeks back then to rest and heal.

The media circled more questions around Dan Pastorini's arm. Columnists wrote bolder assessments and widened their ponderings: Could he really just have a "sore arm" for this long? What is this viral infection that we keep hearing about?

Such questions roused public opinion although there were always people in the public ready to slam Pastorini.

Earlier in the season, Pastorini started battling back. He stopped speaking to *Houston Post* writer Dale Robertson. He felt like Robertson's criticism threatened his livelihood without considering his success in the win column. Pastorini also reminded Robertson that during losing seasons he was one of the few Oilers happy to share quotes with him.

Pastorini, of course, also was extremely popular with many fans and received other positive press in the Houston media.

As for the Oilers players themselves, there didn't seem to be any questions surrounding Pastorini. He quarterbacked the team before many of them got to Houston. They witnessed his toughness and watched him play with broken bones. Houston players fought alongside Pastorini in the trenches and gave him the ultimate support NFL players can give a teammate – trust and respect.

The New York Jets came into the Astrodome throwing. Quarterback Richard Todd and star receiver Wesley Walker likely watched inspirational footage of Steve Largent carving up the Oiler defense. Walker scorched Houston early, snatching receptions of 20 and 39 yards on the first possession. The 39 yarder was a touchdown that put the Jets ahead, 7-0.

Wesley Walker led the AFC in yards per catch his first two seasons. He also led the NFL in receiving yards in 1978. Coming into the Astrodome, he averaged almost 25 yards per catch in 1979.

With the score 7-3 in the second quarter, Walker pulled in a 22-yard catch to set up a field goal and a 10-3 Jets lead. Walker already totaled 111 yards on the day.

Walker suffered a knee sprain in the second quarter, however. The injury knocked him out of the game and sidelined him for the rest of the season. The Jets offense stalled without him.

The Houston offense moved backward. A pair of holding calls forced the Oilers into a first-and-35 situation. Many teams would shrug their shoulders and concede to punting the ball. Not the 1979 Oilers.

Two completions to Mike Renfro helped convert the first down. Rob Carpenter later capped the unlikely drive with a touchdown.

Earl Campbell scored on the Oilers' next possession. Houston recovered from early trouble and led 17-10 at halftime.

A few boos soared down from the Astrodome seats. This was kind of strange, as the Oilers took a lead into the locker room.

The rest of the crowd, however, created the atmosphere known as "Luv Ya Blue." Fans waved pom-poms and danced and sang to the Oilers fight song called, "Houston Oilers Number One." Houston's cheerleaders, the Derrick Dolls, encouraged the noise level.

The NFL hasn't seen anything like Astrodome Sundays before or since.

In the third quarter, the Oilers faced a third-and-4. They handed the ball to 34, and Earl picked up 12 yards.

Pastorini and Barber followed up with a 37-yard touchdown. The touchdown came on a play-action pass, illustrating how Houston exploited defenses needing to respect Campbell's rushing threat.

Houston owned a comfortable 24-10 lead in the fourth quarter. Both Campbell and Bethea left the game after their injuries stiffened. The Oilers two touchdown lead seemed safe, especially considering it was at home. Yet through the Columbia blue cheers, a few boos could still be heard.

Then things started to resemble the game against St. Louis. A couple of special teams mishaps cleared the runway for the Jets offense to take off.

A short punt put the ball at the Oiler 42. Quarterback Richard Todd soon hit Wesley Walker's replacement for an 18-yard score.

Houston's next punt produced even worse results. An interference penalty on the fair catch landed the Jets at the Houston 26. New York drove to the 1-yard line with 55 seconds remaining in the game. Richard Todd called a quarterback sneak and scored a game-tying touchdown.

A few minutes earlier, the Oilers appeared on their way to almost certain victory. Now, the Oilers were on their way to overtime.

Back then, overtime was called "sudden death." Whoever scored first, won. It didn't matter if it was a field goal or a touchdown. Much excitement came from wondering if the defense could stop the team that won the coin toss from getting a few first downs and a field goal.

The Oilers won the toss. Could they get within striking distance?

The Jets defense forced a third down. Pastorini hit Rob Carpenter with a 22-yard screen pass to convert, but the stingy Jets then forced a third-and-10.

Mike Barber caught the ball just short of the marker, but his extra efforts knocked the defense back and he made 12 yards on the play. The drive carried on.

Toni Fritsch soon lined up for a 35-yard field goal. Up and good! Houston won, 27-24, and it was all cheers in the Astrodome.

At the time, Toni Fritsch held the NFL's all-time field goal percentage record. Fritsch grew up in Austria and played professional soccer. The Dallas Cowboys brought the pudgy 5-foot, 7-inch kicker to America in 1971.

Fritsch, who spoke four languages, joined the Oilers in 1977. Bum Phillips used to joke that Fritsch was so good that he sometimes practiced missing field goals.

When asked about the pressure of hitting the game-winning field goal against New York, Fritsch told reporters that he didn't understand the question because there was no word for "pressure" in his native Austrian tongue.

Jets head coach Walt Michaels said that the Jets inability to stop the Oilers on third down made the difference in the game. Houston's third down conversions in overtime proved his statement.

Both Cleveland and Pittsburgh won their games, so this was a very important Oiler win. The victory kept the Oilers tied with Cleveland for second in the AFC Central, one game behind Pittsburgh.

The loss basically knocked the Jets out of the playoff hunt.

Next up for Houston stood the Miami Dolphins in their storied Orange Bowl on *Monday Night Football*.

CHAPTER 13
Week 10 – AT MIAMI

The booing during the Jets game was written about in Houston papers and the *New York Times*. Pastorini was surprised to learn the boos were aimed at him. "I thought they were booing the other team," he replied.

The practice of booing starting quarterbacks isn't unique to Houston. Dallas fans booed Troy Aikman and prompted Roger Staubach to reportedly say that, "Cowboy fans love you win or tie." Dolphins fans booed Dan Marino at one point. Philadelphia Eagles fans, well, they even booed Santa Claus in 1968.

The quarterback position sits squarely at the team's focal point. The head coach also resides there, but Bum was too revered to draw the ire that most head coaches receive. Still, the wise Phillips liked to quip that there were only two types of head coaches, "Them's that's fired and them's that's gonna get fired."

The Oilers selected Pastorini third overall in the 1971 NFL Draft, so he immediately drew a lot of attention. He made a fair amount of money by 1979 NFL standards and his salary brightened the spotlight. He also was a handsome guy who liked to have a good time. Add into the mix that critics weren't going to split time disparaging Bum Phillips and you have a recipe for a hot dish of critical rampage to land on one man's shoulders. In this case, it was Dan Pastorini's throwing shoulder.

Again, it's important to note that not all fans and writers criticized Pastorini. Still, despite the Oilers 6-3 record, a fan-penned letter to the editor bemoaned the fact that Houston fans would never know what might have been if Pastorini wasn't the starting quarterback. The fan closed the critique by writing, "Maybe next year."

A Houston sports columnist who called himself a "Pastorini defender" swiftly altered course in his article by asking if the Oilers had gone as far as they could with Pastorini. Another columnist called the Oilers season "disappointing." He balanced it out by noting that the Oilers could be dangerous in the playoffs if they indeed found a way to get there.

What might have been written if the Oilers had lost to the Jets rather than put a realistic end to New York's playoff chances?

The Oilers didn't have time to ponder such questions. The Miami Dolphins appeared next on their schedule.

The Dolphins sported the best run defense in the National Football League, although Earl Campbell was the last running back to rush for 100 yards against the Dolphins.

That feat was accomplished in the Astrodome in 1978, during what *Monday Night Football* announcer Howard Cosell described as one of the best *Monday Night Football* games in history. Campbell embarrassed the Dolphins with 199 yards rushing and 4 touchdowns in Houston's thrilling 35-30 victory.

ABC hyped the 1979 game as a rematch of the previous year's contest. Miami sat tied with New England for first place in the AFC

East. Excited fans wondered if the Dolphins could score revenge on the Oilers after Houston beat them on *Monday Night Football* and in the playoffs in 1978.

NFL insiders wondered how Earl Campbell might fare on the road against the Dolphins. The last running back to rush for 100 yards against the Dolphins in the Orange Bowl was Baltimore's Joe Washington in October of 1978. You would have to go all the way back to the 1976 season to find another game that Miami allowed a running back to gain 100 yards in the Orange Bowl.

The Dolphins, like the Oilers, suffered injury problems in 1979. Star running back Delvin Williams was out. Williams collected almost 100 all-purpose yards and scored a touchdown against Houston the previous season. Williams finished third amongst AFC rushers in 1978. Williams grew up in Houston, playing high school football at Houston's Kashmere High.

Gary Davis started in Williams' place and had performed well in previous games.

The pressure was on both teams to win. Pittsburgh and Cleveland both won that Sunday. The Oilers needed to keep from sliding a game behind Cleveland and two behind Pittsburgh. The Dolphins needed to hold their ground with New England after the Patriots set the pace by winning their game against Buffalo.

Houston encountered adversity early in the game against the Dolphins. Tight end Mike Barber went down with a serious knee injury. Barber torched Miami's defense the previous season with 112 yards in the playoffs. He also scored a touchdown in the Monday night thriller. He wouldn't be a factor in this game.

A gusty wind backed Miami in the first quarter. The Oilers experienced difficulty throwing into it – and punting into it. A short punt midway through the first quarter started a Dolphin drive at the Houston 41.

Gary Davis pushed them to the 25. Larry Csonka pounded to the Oiler 15. Rookie kicker Uwe von Schamann pounded a field goal.

Trailing 3-0 into the stiff wind, Houston turned to Earl Campbell. He picked up one first down. Then, another first down.

The second quarter began, and the wind turned to Houston's favor. Toni Fritsch kicked a game-tying field goal to cap the drive.

Both teams followed with promising drives that yielded no points.

The Dolphins missed two scoring chances. Oiler defensive back Willie Alexander broke up a pass to Duriel Harris in the end zone. Curley Culp later forced Gary Davis to fumble. Robert Brazile recovered for Houston.

The Oiler drive ended with a missed field goal.

So far, the game looked nothing like 1978's high-scoring affair. Oiler defensive coordinator Ed Biles said that both coaching staffs spent a lot of time watching film of that game to understand why their teams gave up so much yardage. He said they learned each other's offensive tendencies. Both defenses made great adjustments.

The first five minutes of the third quarter went Houston's way. The defense backed Miami up into a fourth-and-30 situation, sparked by a Ken Kennard sack.

The Oiler offense kept it on the ground. Earl for 7. Tim Wilson for 5. Earl for 23, his longest run of the season so far. Toni Fritsch added 3 points with a 48-yard field goal, giving Houston a 6-3 lead.

Oiler linebacker Ted Washington returned for this game, and Elvin Bethea felt better. They teamed up for a third-quarter sack of Dolphin quarterback Bob Griese. Elvin also stuffed a running play.

Houston got the ball back. The Dolphin defense got fed another dose of Campbell. He took the ball three straight times.

On the third run, Campbell landed on top of the first down marker. The first down markers weren't the soft, padded orange sticks of today. Many first down markers of the 70s were metal posts. Earl hit the post so hard that it bent. Earl, who slammed into the bench on a previous run, briefly left the game. Tim Wilson took over and ran to the Dolphin 25, setting up another Toni Fritsch field goal.

Houston led, 9-3, as the third quarter expired. Von Schamann hit a 51-yard field goal early in the fourth to make it 9-6.

This wasn't a pretty game. It didn't pan out to be the thriller fans expected. There was some excitement late, however.

Miami's defense slowed Houston's offense in the fourth quarter. Facing a heavy wind didn't help the Oilers.

Although Miami's defense stymied Houston's offense, Houston's defense forced turnovers.

The Dolphins tried to harness the wind and went for victory on a long pass to receiver Nat Moore. Vernon Perry busted their plans and snagged his first NFL interception.

The Dolphins drove into Houston territory on their next possession. Curley Culp stripped Gary Davis, forcing his second fumble of the game. Robert Brazile recovered the loose ball. The play was an encore performance of a first-half Davis fumble forced by Culp and recovered by Brazile.

Miami started a last-chance drive on their own 16. They got a nice run from Larry Csonka and a nice break on a pass interference call that put them at Houston's 40. On the ensuing third down, running back Tony Nathan caught Bob Griese's pass and darted all the way to the Houston 20.

Miami looked poised to tie the game or take the lead.

Griese faded back and spotted Gary Davis open downfield. He threw a tight spiral on target.

Oiler linebacker Gregg Bingham read the play perfectly. He reached for the ball with outstretched hands and intercepted the pass. He broke loose down the sideline and returned the ball to the Miami 32.

Bingham talked about what he saw on the play. "The way you read (a play) is very important. On that play, the halfback was running a circle route. It was obvious to me that if I could bait him and let Bob (Griese) think he could get it in there, then I could sneak up and get in front of it. And I did."

Bingham made a fine catch on the play, showing better hands than most linebackers. He developed those hands playing tight end in high school.

Notre Dame actually recruited Bingham as a tight end. Bingham then saw Norte Dame tight end Dave Casper. He noted Casper's receiving talents but was even more impressed with his devastating blocking skills. Bingham took a scholarship at Purdue instead, figuring he'd get more playing time.

Bingham's interception marked the third time in the game that the Oilers crushed a fourth-quarter Miami scoring threat with a turnover. The turnovers secured the 9-6 Oiler victory.

The win highlighted the power of Houston's defense. Jesse Baker led the NFL in sacks and Mike Reinfeldt led the league in interceptions. In this game, however, Curley Culp, Robert Brazile, Elvin Bethea, Vernon Perry, Gregg Bingham, and Ted Washington teamed up for the turnovers and sacks. Another win as a defensive family.

After the game, Culp told reporters it was by far the best game the defense played all year. Bethea said the defense came of age. The Oilers outperformed one the NFL's best defenses and did it on the opposing team's own soil.

Toni Fritsch also took his place on the hero's stage, providing all 9 of Houston's points. For the second straight week, and the fourth time that season, Fritsch's foot provided the winning difference on the scoreboard.

The offense only scored 9 points. Pastorini threw only 10 times and netted a mere 25 yards passing. Woeful numbers.

Comparing those numbers with other opponents, however, reveals a gritty offensive effort. The Dolphins had only given up 11 touchdowns all season. No team outside of the AFC East had scored more than 16 points against Miami. Earl Campbell became the first rusher to gain 100 yards against the Dolphins in 1979, and the first opposing back to do so at Miami since October of 1978.

Perhaps the most telling statistic was that Houston ran 58 offensive plays without a single turnover. It was the first time a visiting team prevented a Miami takeaway in the Orange Bowl in nearly five seasons.

CHAPTER 14

Week 11 – HOME VS. OAKLAND

The Oilers held a 7-3 record, tied with Cleveland for second place in the AFC Central, one game behind the 8-2 Steelers. The Steelers and Cowboys both held the best records in football, and both still loomed on the Oilers' schedule.

Bum Phillips fielded more Pastorini-based questions during the week. Reporters pointed to his 25-yard passing total against Miami and asked why he didn't throw more. Some pressed for more information about his arm injury.

Phillips assured everyone that if the Oilers needed more passing yards to beat Miami, then Pastorini would have thrown more passes.

Opinions started to mix. Some looked at stat sheets and questioned Pastorini's lackluster statistics. After all, 25 yards passing in one game and 49 in another were stats that quarterbacks might collect on a single play.

The most important stat, of course, sat inside the win column. Those low passing totals resulted in wins. Seven wins put the Oilers ahead of many teams.

Quarterback Ken Stabler's Oakland Raiders owned 6 wins coming into the Astrodome. Stabler led the Raiders to victory in Super Bowl 11 after the 1976 season.

The Raiders rode into the Astrodome on a hot streak, winning 5 of their last 6 games. They had beaten the Oilers 10 out of the last 11 times the teams they met.

Houston needed to adjust to the loss of tight end Mike Barber. Thankfully, Phillips also had Rich Caster on the roster. Caster was another one of those guys that played well at two positions. He played receiver and tight end. In fact, Caster earned multiple Pro Bowl nominations at tight end with the New York Jets.

Houston's offense heavily featured two offensive formations that week. One formation positioned three receivers on one side – Burrough wide, Renfro in the slot, Caster in tight. The other used two tight ends with two receivers and one running back.

Of course, the biggest question for the Radier defense was, "How do you stop Earl Campbell?"

The short answer is that they couldn't.

The Oilers drove to the 1-yard line in the first quarter. Houston then ran Earl to the right side. He weaved past diving Hall of Fame linebacker Ted Hendricks and approached safety Jack Tatum, one of the hardest hitters in the NFL.

Tatum landed a brutal hit on Campbell. He planted his helmet near Campbell's neck and jawline, driving the crown into Campbell's facemask. Tatum grabbed Campbell's shoulder pads to throw him down.

Campbell turned his back to the end zone and staggered diagonally over the goal line. The Oilers led 7-0 after one of the greatest 1-yard runs in NFL history.

Campbell's shorter runs were often magical. Some players looked like they ran five yards to pick up two. Earl sometimes looked like he picked up only two yards, but it turned out that he picked up four or five. He was that quick to the line, that strong, and that difficult to bring down.

While the Raiders focused on Earl Campbell, Dan Pastorini focused on how the Raiders' double zone defense matched up against the Oilers passing game. Pastorini noted that Campbell's running threat froze Oakland linebackers on passing plays. He also recognized Oiler receivers could beat the Raider secondary deep and down the middle.

He called Double-0's number in the second quarter with the score tied at 7. He laced a 55-yard dart on first down. Kenny Burrough caught it in stride. Touchdown, Oilers.

The Astrodome rocked. Columbia blue pom-poms bobbed in the air. Pastorini's fastball was back. The arm started to feel like its old self.

The Raiders tied the game at 14 by halftime, but the Oiler offense developed an explosive mixture of superstar running back and dynamite throwing arm. The Oilers and the crowd hit ignition and readied for lift off.

Houston soared in the second half. Pastorini hit Burrough for another long touchdown, this one for 35 yards. He hit Mike Renfro for chunks of 47 and 36 yards. Tim Wilson got into the act with a 7-yard touchdown run.

Wilson was so excited that he lofted the ball into the stands, a $100 fine at the time.

The defense squelched the Raiders in the second half. Mike Reinfeldt snared two interceptions, getting revenge on the team that placed him on waivers.

The $100 waiver wire fee Houston paid to acquire Reinfeldt looked like a genius investment. Reinfeldt now had 11 interceptions on the year, just three shy of Dick "Night Train" Lane's all-time record of 14.

The Oilers' 31-17 win was the second straight over a perennial AFC playoff contender and their third straight overall.

More importantly, the win launched them over Cleveland in the divisional standings, as the Browns fell to the streaking Seattle Seahawks. The Steelers remained in first place, a game ahead of Houston. Oiler fans circled their Week 15 game against Pittsburgh in the Astrodome.

Campbell totaled over 100 yards against Oakland and surpassed 1,000 for the season. The accomplishment made him the first AFC player in history to total 1,000 rushing yards for each of his first two seasons.

Pastorini looked as good as ever and his arm felt better than it had all season. Bum Phillips told reporters after the game that Dan's arm was about where it would normally be late in preseason.

Pastorini pointed out that although he posted outstanding numbers on his personal stat sheet against the Raiders, a lot of players with big stats lose games. Winning is what mattered most.

Winning always mattered most to Raiders owner Al Davis. His motto for the team was, "Just win, baby."

Davis almost certainly took note of Pastorini's performance that week in the Astrodome.

CHAPTER 15

Week 12 – HOME VS. CINCINNATI

The win over Oakland excited fans and writers alike. The sports columns talked more about playoff possibilities than what the Oilers did wrong. Letters to the editor defended Pastorini. One columnist who regularly questioned Pastorini's arm strength now wrote that he seemed as good as ever.

What a difference a week makes in the NFL.

The lowly Cincinnati Bengals came to town in Week 12. Oiler fans looked ahead to the next week, a Thanksgiving Day game at Dallas.

The team needed to stay focused on the Bengals after Cincinnati pounded the Steelers 34-10 and built up a 24-point lead against the Oilers in Week 4. The Bengals also led playoff-bound San Diego until the final seconds in Week 10.

The Oilers had won three straight, whereas the Bengals had only won two games the entire season. Bum Phillips always said you should win the games you should win, split the games against teams as good as you, and let the chips fall where they may. The Bengal game fell into the "should win" category.

Houston's defense came into the game with more sacks than they tallied in all of 1978. Jesse Baker played a large part in that. The rookie led the way with 14 ½ sacks.

Elvin Bethea discusses Baker's talent: "He was so strong. I mean, he would just take a guy, grab him by his shoulder pads, and just drive him straight back into the quarterback, just bullrush over a guy.

"I made sure that I tried to pass on what I had, what I experienced, and my play to him. I said, 'Jesse, you have to use some technique. Get the guy moving. Get his feet moving. Get him going where he doesn't want to go.'

"He caught on quick.

"He was just a laid-back guy, but when it was time to come out and play or practice, either one, that offensive tackle had his hands full."

Surprisingly, Houston entered the game with Mike Barber, who decided to postpone season-ending surgery. He sucked it up, as many players did in those days. His love for his teammates and Coach Phillips motivated him to stay on the field.

"They taped it up for me," Barber said. "It took me a while to loosen up, but I was able to get my mind off of it. But that's how players were in those days. Today, you sprain an ankle and you're out for four weeks. There were a lot of players on our team, as well as other teams, who sucked it up. We played injured and hurt."

Early in the game, Houston picked up where they left off against Oakland and quickly answered any questions about overlooking the Bengals.

Two rushing touchdowns – one by Campbell and one by Carpenter – tacked a 14-0 lead onto the scoreboard. After Pastorini hit Barber for a 17-yard touchdown in the second quarter, the Oilers led, 21-7.

Barber, who ran the high hurdles in college, ran fast for a tight end. Bum drafted him in the first round of the 1976 draft and said, "I don't know if he can block, but he sure can run."

Barber talked about how he got open and credited Earl Campbell's running threat.

"I was blessed with pretty good speed and when you got a running back in the backfield like we had, it really made those strong safeties and free safeties bite real hard on play-action. If I could be running pretty much at top speed, and get right beside him (a defender), I had pretty good fortune in getting over the top of him and getting into the open."

He added that having great teammates like Ken Burrough and the rest of the Oiler receiving corps helped.

"I got a lot of Cover 2 – two safeties watching those guys over the top. That left me pretty open in the middle, just one-on-one with a linebacker. And I could win most of those battles."

Pastorini had things humming again, but adversity struck once more. Bengal defensive lineman Eddie Edwards busted through the line. Pastorini ducked. Edwards swatted his hand toward Pastorini's face. His thumb smashed into Pastorini's left eye.

"I ducked down to kind of get under him," Pastorini said. "He reached down, brought his hand up, and his thumb went right into my left eye. I couldn't open my eye. I really thought my eye was popped out, that my eye was gone. Fortunately, there was an eye doctor in the stadium who came down and looked at it. He said, 'You have a scratched cornea.'"

Gifford Nielsen came in at quarterback. The offensive linemen encouraged him. They told him in the huddle to keep things going.

Nielsen responded and completed his first six passes. The Oilers led 35-7 at halftime. Earl Campbell got to rest the entire second half. Houston coasted to a 42-21 win in a game they should have won.

The Astrodome scoreboard said, "We Want Dallas!" Fans chanted the scoreboard's words.

Meanwhile, Cleveland edged Miami in overtime. Pittsburgh, however, got thumped 35-7 at San Diego.

The Chargers put the league on notice that they expected to go deep into the playoffs. San Diego quarterback Dan Fouts said, "We know we'll see the Steelers again down the road."

That remained to be seen. For now, the Chargers did the Oilers a favor, and Houston moved back up into a first-place tie with Pittsburgh in the AFC Central.

Next up, the Dallas Cowboys at Texas Stadium on Thanksgiving Day. The Chargers, the Steelers, and everybody else in America would be watching.

CHAPTER 16

Week 13 – AT DALLAS

They were called, "America's Team."

NFL Films produced a highlight reel commemorating the Cowboy's 1978 season and christened the Cowboys, "America's Team."

The title stuck. For most opponents it became a call to action, "Let's beat America's Team." The moniker also gave opposing fans one more reason to cheer against the Cowboys.

Dallas frustrated many teams' fans by winning. In the 1970s, Dallas won Super Bowls 6 and 12, and played in Super Bowls 5, 10, and 13. Since the merger, the Cowboys hogged the majority of NFC championships. Minnesota grabbed three, and Washington, one. The Cowboys owned the rest. No other NFC team caught a whiff of the Super Bowl entering the 1979 season.

Houston fans owned another reason to dislike the Cowboys. The Oilers were the "other" team in Texas, viewed by some as a small-time operation compared to the Cowboys' empire.

A large number of Cowboys fans lived in Houston, to the chagrin of Oiler players and fans. In fact, enough Cowboys fans lived in Houston that the *Houston Chronicle* kept a writer on staff to cover the Dallas Cowboys.

Carl Mauck particularly took offense to Cowboys fans living in Houston, telling them to head up I-45 and move to the Metroplex. He even offered to help them move. Elvin Bethea heard that and offered to pitch in as well.

The Thanksgiving Day game against the Cowboys was billed as the "Texas Super Bowl." Since the teams weren't in the same conference, the game didn't matter as much in the playoff standings as the divisional matchup the Oilers had just won against Cincinnati.

Still, the game meant a ton to Oiler fans. A win over Dallas on a national stage, especially in Dallas, would likely stack up as one of the sweetest-tasting regular season wins in team history.

The Oiler players were keenly aware of this. Elvin Bethea was quoted as saying that although the game didn't mean as much as a divisional game, it meant a lot to the fans and therefore meant a lot to the team.

A win wouldn't just make a statement for the fans. It would make a statement to the NFL that the Houston Oilers were indeed for real. A win would also mark the first time that the Oilers beat the Cowboys during the regular season.

Dallas head coach Tom Landry kept things complicated with an offense littered with trick plays and multiple formations. The defense also was confusing. Landry created what was called the "flex defense" which at times even confused his own players. Players ran to certain areas of the field for which they were responsible, not necessarily in pursuit of the ball or an offensive player.

Landry also used a computer to help analyze teams' tendencies. The computer spit out how often teams ran a certain play on third down or what plays they ran from a certain field position.

Few approached the game that way in the 1970s, and Landry was often mocked for using computers. Landry was way ahead of the times in that regard. You now see computer tablets on the sidelines during games.

Thanksgiving, of course, always falls on a Thursday. That gave the Oilers only four days to prepare for the complex Cowboys. Bum Phillips, always clever in his comments, said he didn't mind a short week as long as the Oilers didn't have a long afternoon.

Both Houston and Dallas stood tied for first place in their respective divisions. The game might not have mattered as much in a playoff tiebreaker setting, but it still meant quite a bit in terms of staying in first place.

A win also meant a lot of pride. Especially if Houston managed to beat American's Team in their own stadium on Thanksgiving with America watching.

Carl Mauck stepped out on the field for warmups. He heard "The Wabash Cannonball" playing. He figured that was a good omen for the Oiler Cannonball to crash through Texas Stadium.

The stadium looked kind of like an unfinished dome. An oblong-shaped hole opened over the playing surface and fully exposed players to the elements. The stadium's seats, however, were mostly shielded from the sun and rain.

Dallas received the opening kickoff and drove to their own 44, as star running back Tony Dorsett and fullback Robert Newhouse carried the ball with success.

Quarterback Roger Staubach knew what to do next. He faked to Dorsett on a first-down play-action pass. He sent his favorite deep threat, Drew Pearson, on a fly pattern.

Pearson sprinted straight down the field and raced past the man-to-man coverage. Staubach floated a perfectly thrown ball to Pearson. Pearson crossed the goal line for a touchdown as easy as Thanksgiving gravy.

The Cowboys led by 7, less than two minutes into the game. Dallas fans cheered loudly and excitedly, hoping that it would indeed be a long afternoon for Bum Phillips and his team.

The Oilers lined up at their own 30 after Carter Hartwig's kick-off return.

Dan Pastorini removed an eye patch before the game, and a harsh glare stared him in the face as he lined up under center. His scratched cornea intensified the bright sunrays like a mirror. The glare affected his vision and amplified the pain. He couldn't wait for the sun to drift beneath Texas Stadium's partial roof.

Earl Campbell took the ball on first down. He almost broke into the open field but slipped after a short gain. Pastorini then hit Mike Barber in the flat for about five yards.

Houston faced a third-and-1.

Pastorini walked to the line of scrimmage and noticed the strong safety lined up to his left. The alignment told him to run Earl Campbell to the right side. He figured if Earl got through the line of scrimmage on the right side, the play would probably gain at least 10 yards. An easy first down if nothing else.

Center Carl Mauck snapped the ball. Pastorini handed it to Campbell. Barber burst off the line to shove linebacker D.D. Lewis. Guard Ed Fisher pulled and blocked linebacker Bob Bruenig. Those blocks created a crease on the right side.

Lewis spun away from Barber, but the speedy Campbell was already gone -- 10 yards past the line of scrimmage.

Earl turned the corner.

He needed to outrun free safety Cliff Harris to the outside. Like Neil Armstrong racing against the Wright Brothers, Earl rocketed past Harris and bolted across midfield. Cornerback Aaron Kyle desperately dove at Earl's heels but caught nothing but Campbell's exhaust.

Earl ran the final 20 yards by himself, as easily as running sprints after practice.

From liftoff to touchdown, the Cowboys didn't stand a chance on the play. Pastorini discusses how Earl Campbell's greatness and the simplicity of King Hill's offensive designs supercharged the play.

"I go up to the line of scrimmage and I look at their defense. I go, 'Where are you going to declare strength?' They have to put their strong safety somewhere.

"If they put him over Barber to the right, then I'd call plays to the left. If they put him over Rich Caster on the left, then I'd call plays to the right. They (the defense) couldn't be right. They were never right.

"That's where our offense helped because I could spend time at the line of scrimmage and look at what the alignments were so we never ran Earl into a bad situation. We always gave Earl a crease, and if you gave him a crease of about 18 inches, he could bust it through. And the likelihood of him running over a cornerback or a safety was on our side."

The touchdown exemplified the greatness of Earl Campbell.

The blocking set up what likely would have been a short run for a first down by a good NFL running back. A Pro-Bowl caliber back might have gained 10 yards, as Cowboy free safety Cliff Harris and two others owned good tackling angles about 10 yards downfield. Earl Campbell's speed and power vaulted him 10 yards downfield faster than most backs in NFL history, and well ahead of the Cowboys' defense.

The Oilers took the Cowboys' lightning quick punch to the jaw on Drew Pearson's touchdown and countered with their own. Campbell's 61-yard dash told Dallas that Houston wasn't going to back down, and the quick response told America that this Thanksgiving would present a special game with outstanding players making exceptional plays. Complete with all the fixings.

Houston's defense experienced difficulty stopping the Cowboys on third down. Dallas drove to Houston's 17 before a holding call set up a second-and-15.

Now it was Roger Staubach's turn to read the defense.

He lifted a screen pass to Robert Newhouse over a slew of Oilers blitzing the pocket. That left Newhouse running behind three blockers with only two Oilers to beat. He barely had to make a cut and scored easily. 14-7, Dallas.

The Oilers kicked a field goal early in the second quarter after a Vernon Perry interception. Ken Burrough suffered an injury on the drive and his return was questionable.

Dallas' offense continued to find success on third down. The Cowboys responded with a touchdown drive increase their lead to 21-10. The Oilers trailed by 11 points.

Houston also trailed by 11 at Washington, but the Cowboys – Roger Staubach, Tom Landry, the Doomsday Defense – they were a much taller task. Houston needed another score before halftime or risk that long afternoon Bum Phillips feared.

Rich Ellender returned the kickoff to the Houston 23 with about five minutes left in the first half.

Defensive linemen John Dutton and Larry Cole smothered Campbell for a 3-yard loss on first down. Dutton, a former star for the Colts, had just come to Dallas in a trade and was making his first start for the Cowboys.

Pastorini dropped back on second down. Harvey Martin waved his huge arm in Pastorini's face, and it looked like a sure sack. Leon Gray fought Martin off with his great strength, however, and shoved Martin aside. Pastorini threw a strike to Rich Caster for 29 yards -- a good piece of yardage towards a field goal, and a first down at the Oiler 49.

That play showed how an offensive lineman can affect a drive. A lesser tackle would have likely allowed a sack, making it third-and-15 or perhaps even more. Instead, the play gained 29 yards.

Houston kept the drive alive with a nice second-down run by Tim Wilson and a third-down catch by Mike Renfro.

Classic Campbell followed.

He grabbed a pitchout to the left. He weaved inside Tim Wilson's block. He then cut sharply left, causing linebacker Mike Hegman to fall. He quickly moved inside a step and jumped over Aaron Kyle. Linebacker Bob Bruenig caught Campbell's shoe as he landed.

Earl stumbled forward for more yardage before Cliff Harris took advantage of Earl's unsteady momentum and brought him down. Had Bruenig not barley caught Earl's shoestrings, Campell might have scored his second touchdown of the day.

The run put Houston within striking distance, on the Cowboy 30 with just over two minutes left in the first half.

The drive was exactly what the Oilers needed, and the offense pitched in as a family: a crucial block by Leon Gray; clutch catches by Caster and Renfro; on the money throws by Pastorini.

And of course, Earl Campbell.

The ball rested on the right hashmark before second down. The spot granted a bit more space toward the left side of the field. Receiver Guido Merkens ran in motion toward the right sideline, hoping to bring a defender with him.

The offensive line got a huge push off the snap and knocked the entire Cowboy line backwards. Center Carl Mauck pulled to the left.

Earl took the handoff and got to the line of scrimmage with his entire offensive line still in front of him. Conway Hayman sealed off Campbell's right side. Mauck, Leon Gray, and Rich Caster sealed off his left side.

Campbell exploded through the hole. Cliff Harris again chased Campbell across the field, but his valiant efforts failed. Campbell raced past Harris, who dove at nothing but air.

Earl blew into the end zone for a 27-yard touchdown, this time running the last 12 yards by himself.

Excellent blocking, a Hall of Fame running back, sure-handed receivers, an experienced quarterback calling plays, and an offense designed for on-the-fly changes put the Oilers in position to come back on the road once again.

One big question remained: Could the Oiler defense find a way to stop Roger Staubach, Tony Dorsett, Drew Pearson, and the rest of Dallas' high-octane offense from scoring?

Almost two minutes remained in the first half for the Oiler defense to provide their first answer.

In each of the Oilers' comebacks during '78 and '79, Houston played shutdown defense in the second half. This time, the defense needed to quell one of the most potent and complex offenses of the 1970s on the road, against one of the best NFL quarterbacks to come in many generations.

The drive didn't start out so well for the Columbia Blue. Dallas started on their own 34 and Staubach immediately threw for 10 yards. On the next play, he tossed a swing pass to Dorsett. Dorsett fooled a couple of would-be tacklers and got inside the Oiler 40.

Tony Dorsett and Earl Campbell were both great runners with different styles. Dorsett made tacklers miss with shifty moves and great agility. Campbell also had great agility but fortified it with incredible strength. Campbell punished tacklers. If Dorsett ran like a deer, then Campbell ran like a bull. Both are in the Pro Football Hall of Fame.

The Cowboys offense cut up the Oiler defense like many viewers tore through their pumpkin pie. Piece by piece, Dallas chewed up yardage. The Cowboys called their first time out with 1:15 left, on the cusp of kicker Rafael Septien's field goal range.

Curley Culp had seen enough. The next play came his way and he slammed Preston Pearson to the turf for a 4-yard loss.

Staubach then found receiver Tony Hill open for first down yardage, but Mike Reinfeldt knocked Hill out of bounds as he juggled the ball.

On third down it was strong safety Vernon Perry's turn.

Staubach called for a pass to tight end Jay Saldi. The play spread the defense to the sidelines, leaving Saldi one-on-one with Perry. Perry covered Saldi like a blanket and knocked the pass down.

Gregg Bingham talked about how Perry strengthened the Oiler defense from the strong safety position.

"Vernon Perry was a tremendous find for us. We made Vernon a strong safety.

"Since he had so much (experience) at cornerback, he could cover the tight end one-on-one. We didn't have to worry about (the tight end) because Vernon could cover him.

"If Vernon could take the tight end away, then you could put in your nickel and your right corner would double the wide receiver with the weak (free) safety. The left corner could take away the z-receiver, with my underneath help. You'd have everybody doubled that way, except the tight end, and Vernon could cover the tight end one-on-one."

Dallas led 21-17 at halftime. Campbell had 122 yards rushing and two touchdowns in the first half. Staubach had over 200 yards passing.

The Oilers started with the ball in the second half. Earl Campbell took the ball on the first four plays of the half, and plowed Houston to a first down at the Dallas 47.

Pastorini sent Guido Merkens in motion again, this time running toward the left sideline. Mauck snapped the ball and Dan faked a handoff to Campbell.

Pastorini then pump-faked a throw to Merkens on the sideline. Pastorini dropped back further and saw Mike Renfro all by himself at the 20-yard line. Renfro caught the ball between the numbers, cut toward the middle, and outran three scrambling defenders to the end zone for a score.

The Oilers led, 23-21.

The touchdown was extra special for Renfro. His father once worked as an assistant coach for the Cowboys. Young Mike served as the Cowboys' water boy and played catch with quarterbacks Don Meredith and Craig Morton. Now, here he was on Thanksgiving catching a real NFL touchdown in Dallas.

Unfortunately, Toni Fritsch missed the extra point, leaving the door open for the Cowboys to take the lead with a field goal.

Kenny Burrough started the second half on the trainer's table, as doctors treated him for a broken tailbone. He heard the crowd's loud roar and figured the Cowboys had scored. He returned to the sideline and looked at the scoreboard. By golly, the *Oilers* had scored. The Luv Ya Blue crowd had made its mark in Big D.

The Oilers owned the lead even though Roger Staubach completed 14 of 17 passes in the first half. At one point, he was 11 for 12. Houston took the best punches Dallas could give and held steady on the road.

How many more punches did the Cowboys have? And how many more could the Oilers take?

Staubach quickly hit Drew Pearson for a first down, but something happened on that play and on the incompletion at the end of the first half. Staubach got knocked down after he threw. This time by Curley Culp.

The Oilers blitzed with linebacker Ted Thompson on the Cowboys' second-down play. Thompson, Elvin Bethea, and Andy Dorris all combined for a sack.

The Oiler pass rush got to Staubach again on third down. His hurried throw fell incomplete.

After getting bested on third down for most of the first half, Houston's defense registered two straight stops, one to close the first half and one to open the second half.

Dallas punted, and the Oilers marched downfield again. Houston's offense slowed around the Cowboy 33-yard line. Houston faced a fourth-and-2.

Campbell averaged a ridiculous 5 yards per carry in short-yardage situations. Bum decided to go for it.

Campbell didn't even get to the line of scrimmage. Pastorini and Campbell mishandled the exchange and the ball dropped to the turf. The Oilers recovered but lost the ball on downs.

Dallas took the ball and the momentum.

Momentum makes a difference in every game. It is the difference between running uphill and downhill. Dallas now ran downhill at home.

Tight end Billy Joe DuPree made a big play, busting into Houston territory. Dorsett picked up 12 yards on third-and-2. Dallas had a first down at Houston's 27.

Houston needed to slow Dallas' momentum. Andy Dorris started by tackling Robert Newhouse behind the line of scrimmage.

Staubach then tried a play that scored a touchdown in the first half. He tossed a screen pass over the Oiler pass rush. Tony Dorsett caught the ball with a wall of blockers in front of him.

Robert Brazile got tied up in a block but refused to quit. He pushed the blocker into Dorsett, causing Dorsett to fall. The play lost yardage.

Next, the Oilers easily stopped a third-and-long as the third quarter expired.

Dallas kicked a field goal on the first play of the fourth quarter. The Cowboys owned a 24-23 lead, but Houston's defensive stand slowed Dallas' momentum. Furthermore, Houston could still take the lead with a field goal and an Oiler touchdown would put them ahead by 6 rather than 2.

Ken Burrough's broken tailbone caused him tremendous pain. The cold Thanksgiving weather didn't ease the injury. Such pain has stopped many a player.

Brazile came up to him, "Kenny, if you can go, we need you."

Pastorini echoed. "Kenny, we need you."

Coach Phillips chimed in, "Look Ken, if there's any way you can get out there, we need you."

Burrough courageously stepped onto the field.

The Oilers took over near their own 40-yard line, thanks to the Cowboys twice booting the kickoff out of bounds. The Cowboys forced a punt, but by this time Pastorini noticed an adjustment the Cowboys made during the game.

Free safety Cliff Harris keyed on Earl Campbell. Harris rushed toward the line of scrimmage to support the Cowboys run defense, a scheme designed to limit Campbell. Pastorini made a mental note to exploit that tendency at the right time.

Meanwhile, Staubach went for his own big play.

On first down, he sent receiver Tony Hill on a fly pattern, just like he did with Drew Pearson in the first quarter for an easy touchdown.

This time, however, the Oilers came up big. Cornerback J.C. Wilson, who had played college ball at Pitt with Tony Dorsett, leapt for the ball and came down with the interception at the Houston 33.

Two plays later, Cowboys pass rush charged on third-and-eight. Harvey Martin moved into crush Pastorini.

He swatted Pastorini in the helmet and tried to bring the quarterback down with his strong right arm. Pastorini, however, kept his balance. Martin lost his and fell.

In a split second, Pastorini spotted Mike Barber at midfield and fired a line drive between two Cowboy safeties. Defensive end Larry Bethea and defensive tackle Dave Stalls hit Pastorini just after he released the ball.

The tough Barber, playing through his knee injury, latched on for an 11-yard catch and first down.

Football is a game of inches and split seconds. Had Martin been a few inches closer to Pastorini, he likely would have had enough leverage to record the sack. Two other Cowboys missed the sack by a split-second. The pass sliced through a tight window of Cowboy defenders, an inch from being knocked away.

Pastorini and Barber made great plays on both ends, and the Oilers won a game of inches and split seconds.

Campbell then bullied his way across the 50, dragging several Cowboys with him. Tim Wilson then picked up a first down at the Dallas 43.

Campbell next ran twice and Rob Carpenter once, but to little avail. The drive stalled at the Dallas 39.

Cowboy fans roared. Houston needed a big stop on defense to keep within a field goal.

Cliff Parsley punted for Houston. The ball bounced out of bounds at the 10. A penalty marker lay on the field on the 13. The Cowboys had 12 men on the field.

The costly mistake gave the Oilers five yards and, most importantly, a first down on the Cowboy 32.

Mental errors were not a trademark of Tom Landry's coaching style. Landry kept his cool, but paced back and forth, shaking his head.

Pastorini took the first-down snap and turned toward Campbell. Cliff Harris rushed in from his safety position, but this time it wasn't a running play. It was a play-action pass.

The play-action left Ken Burrough one-on-one with cornerback Benny Barnes, with no coverage help from a safety.

Even with a broken tailbone, Double-0 had speed. He broke loose on a post pattern, a few steps ahead of Barnes.

Standing in the pocket with good protection, Pastorini hit Burrough in stride. Touchdown.

The Oiler fans in the crowd cheered nearly as loud as Cowboy fans did earlier. The Oilers led 30-24 after the extra point.

Now it was up to the defense to hold that lead. Roger Staubach, sometimes referred to as "Captain Comeback," had over seven-and-a-half minutes at his disposal.

The Cowboys drove to their own 46 a minute later. Tony Dorsett caught a screen pass and dodged tackles to pick up a first down.

With five minutes left, Staubach hit Drew Pearson for a first down at the Oiler 36. Houston's pass rush hit Staubach hard after the throw. The defensive line inched closer to a sack as the clock ticked.

Could Houston stop Captain Comeback?

Andy Dorris broke through the line and tackled Dorsett for a loss.

This game meant a lot to Dorris. He lined up against Cowboy tackle Rayfield Wright, nicknamed, "Big Cat." Wright, now a member of the Pro Football Hall of Fame, gave Dorris a lot of problems over the years. Dorris wanted to even the score against the Big Cat in a game that featured personal rivalries on top of the intrastate rivalry.

The Cowboys soon faced a fourth-and-10 from the 36 with three-and-a-half minutes left. Fans for both teams cheered in a loud Texas Stadium.

Staubach hit Tony Hill for a first down at the 20. Tom Landry, famous for never showing emotion on the sidelines, jumped with excitement.

With 2:40 left, Dallas ran Dorsett. He got crushed near the line of scrimmage by a combination Dorris, Brazile, and Bingham.

The Cowboys let the clock run down to the two-minute warning. Staubach knew that if he scored a go-ahead touchdown too early, Earl Campbell and company could drive for a game-winning field goal.

Both teams dodged a bullet on second down.

Staubach threw to Tony Dorsett. The ball ricocheted off Oiler Ted Thompson's hands, and next off Dorsett's hands, who might have scored on the play. When all was said and done, the pass fell incomplete and the Cowboys faced a third-and-9.

Staubach faded back. Tony Hill looked wide open coming across the middle at the goal line.

Hill lunged for a high pass, got a hand on it, but couldn't reel in the touchdown. The ball tumbled harmlessly into the end zone.

Fourth down. The whole country watching. Captain Comeback often thrived under these conditions.

Millions watched Staubach do it before. They saw it in 1975 when the legendary "Hail Mary" pass landed in Drew Pearson's hands to beat Minnesota in the playoffs. He also knocked San Francisco out of the playoffs with a miracle comeback in 1972.

Staubach seemed to pull one out of the hat even more frequently during the regular season. He previously conducted game-winning drives against the Cardinals, Bears, and Giants that season.

How would the Oilers respond?

Staubach dropped back. He scoured the field. The Oiler defense blanketed his receivers. Houston's pass rush closed in on Staubach's left. He looked to run right.

Andy Dorris cut off his path. Dorris closed in unopposed, his massive arms outstretched.

Staubach hurried a throw. The desperate pass landed on a patch of turf, hopelessly out of bounds and out of reach.

Shutdown defense.

Bum Phillips threw his arms in the air. J.C. Wilson jumped up and down with Greg Stemrick. Oiler fans cheered loudly.

The Oilers stood at the top of the NFL's mountain as the first team to 10 wins, and the whole country watched it happen.

Bum Phillips smiled and said, "If Dallas is America's Team, then Houston must be Texas' team."

CHAPTER 17

Week 14 – AT CLEVELAND

Houston rallied from 11 points down to beat Dallas, tied for the largest comeback against the Cowboys at Texas Stadium in the 1970s. Earl Campbell rushed for an astounding 195 yards and two touchdowns. Pastorini threw for two touchdowns and no interceptions. The Oilers had won five straight.

The critics, both of Pastorini and the team, retreated and fell from sight.

Pastorini totaled only two interceptions in those five games. He threw six touchdowns. He was the NFL's second-highest rated passer for Week 13. Campbell was the week's leading rusher. The Oiler passing game now hummed alongside the rushing attack.

And that defense! The Columbia Blue defense caused 45 turnovers thus far, averaging over three per game. The pass rush forced hurried throws. The secondary produced interceptions. The team shutdown great offenses when games hung in the balance.

At 10-3, the Oilers stood tied for first place in the AFC Central and for the best record in the NFL. Their next opponent, the Cleveland Browns, owned an impressive 8-5 record but languished in jeopardy of missing the AFC playoffs.

The Browns played at Pittsburgh on the Sunday after Thanksgiving, and quarterback Brian Sipe ripped the Steeler secondary for the second time that season. Sipe netted over 330 yards and 3 TDs.

Like Pastorini said after the Oakland game, a lot of exciting stats don't equal wins. The Steelers overcame Sipe's brilliant numbers, rallied from 14 points down, and won the game in overtime.

Pittsburgh remained in a first-place tie with Houston. The Browns sank two games behind the leaders.

The upcoming Houston-Cleveland game meant a lot to both teams. For Houston, it meant a chance at winning the division if they beat Cleveland and then Pittsburgh in Week 15. For Cleveland, it meant staying alive in the playoff hunt.

The game marked the Oilers' second straight road game. They played two on the road twice before in 1979, resulting in lopsided losses at Pittsburgh and Seattle. Both of those punishing defeats came after road wins. The Oilers hoped to reverse that trend at Cleveland after winning at Dallas.

A snowy cold front moved into Cleveland. The early December wind whipped off Lake Eerie. The 28-degree weather felt like 17 degrees as the wind blew at 15 miles per hour.

The night before the game, Cleveland running back Mike Pruitt had a dream that the Browns beat the Oilers 42-7.

Cold reality can be another story.

In their Week 5 matchup in Houston, the Oilers jumped out early and had a 24-3 lead in the second quarter. Cleveland head coach Sam Rutigliano sought to avoid that in this game.

The Browns found early success in that quest. Running back Mike Pruitt, having a fine year replacing the injured Gregg Pruitt, snagged a Brian Sipe pass for a 42-yard score in the first quarter. The Browns led, 7-0.

Rutigliano felt bold in the wintery conditions. He called for an onside kick. He hoped to catch the Oilers by surprise. He also wanted to keep Houston's red-hot offense off the field.

The tactic backfired. Ted Thompson recovered the kick for the Oilers. Five plays later, Earl Campbell dashed through the steady snowfall for an 11-yard touchdown. The score was tied at 7 at the end of the first quarter.

The division rivals knew each other well. The combination of the snow and cold and the defenses knowing what to expect limited the offenses. The score remained tied at 7 at halftime.

Bum Phillips hoped to make something happen in the first five minutes of the third quarter, like the Oilers did against Dallas with the Renfro score. The Browns were not hospitable hosts to that plan.

Cleveland engineered a time-consuming drive to start the half. The Browns drove all the way to the Oiler 3-yard line before Greg Stemrick picked off Brian Sipe in the end zone. Stemrick raced all the way to midfield before Sipe pushed him out of bounds, halting a potential touchdown.

The Oilers proceeded to go three-and-out on offense. Those three plays were the only plays Houston ran in the third quarter.

The Browns methodically nudged down the field, grinding time off the clock. Meanwhile, Mike Pruitt became the second AFC rusher to top 1,000 yards for the season, a feat that Campbell accomplished weeks before against Oakland. Cleveland's cautious, time-consuming drive got them a first down at Houston's 24.

Houston's defense prepared for Sipe to utilize his prolific passing skills. On game day, however, the weather limited passing. Sipe took to the ground instead, and his feet proved as damaging as his arm.

Sipe faded back to pass but decided to flee the pocket. He scrambled 9 yards to the 15. He outdid himself on the next play and scrambled 14 yards to the Houston 1. Mike Pruitt took it from there, and the Browns led 14-7 early in the fourth quarter.

Brian Sipe wasn't known as a rushing threat. He rarely dashed from the pocket. In this game, he ran out of necessity and racked up 42 yards on 5 carries, only 1 yard shy of his career best.

Houston responded to the Browns touchdown and drove to the Cleveland 44. Pastorini called for a long pass and was intercepted at the 7.

Houston's defense forced a punt, and the Oilers' final hope started at their own 20-yard line.

The Oilers won a lot of close games by just hanging in there until they finally took the lead. Would this be one of those games?

Behind Campbell's rushing and Pastorini's passing, Houston arrived at the Cleveland 38 with 1:13 left. A pass to Campbell picked up another 15 yards. A game-tying touchdown stood a mere 23 yards away, with 46 seconds left.

On third-and-10, Pastorini again hit Campbell on a screen. A vicious hit by defensive end Lyle Alzado and linebacker Dick Ambrose forced a fumble. The Browns recovered both the ball and their playoff hopes.

Mike Pruitt's dream came partly true. The Browns won, but only by a 14-7 margin.

After the game, Sam Rutigliano said Cleveland's main plan was to run the ball, consume clock, and keep Earl Campbell off the field. He added that they were more successful than they planned. Sipe called it Cleveland's most important win of the year.

A Houston win might have set up next week's clash against Pittsburgh as a division championship game. Instead, the Oilers would have to win that Monday night simply to have hopes of winning the division. The Steelers recorded their 11th win of the season. Bum Phillips simply stated, "We gotta beat Pittsburgh next week and that's all there is to it."

One thing was certain. The dome would be rocking.

CHAPTER 18

Rockin' at the Astrodome

Oiler home games meant a rollicking atmosphere at the Houston Astrodome.

The indoor stadium, originally named Harris County Domed Stadium, opened in 1965. The Oilers didn't play there until 1968.

The Luv Ya Blue era of the Houston Oilers franchise rooted itself with the fans as much as the players. Everything came together at the perfect time, in the perfect place, under one enormous roof.

The "Urban Cowboy" fad, the city's growth, and Houston's winning football team equaled a phenomenon. The NFL, and pro sports in general, has never seen anything like it before or since. Fans raised the decibel meter to new levels, waved pom-poms, and sang and danced to Oiler-themed songs. "Houston Oilers Number One" topped the charts as the most famous Oiler fight song.

Esquire documented the Urban Cowboy lifestyle in September of 1978. The story followed the life of a Pasadena, Texas refinery worker who spent his nights at Gilley's nightclub. Paramount Pictures immediately bought the movie rights.

The movie *Urban Cowboy*, starring John Travolta, started filming in Houston in July of 1979, just as the Oilers started training camp. Western wear and country western music rose in popularity across the U.S. at the same time the Oilers climbed the standings.

Bum Phillips stood on the sidelines in a cowboy hat and boots. A Hollywood casting director could not have found a better leading man. Phillips lived on a ranch, raised cattle, and befriended country music stars like Willie Nelson and Larry Gatlin.

Earl Campbell was added to the cast in 1978. He was born and raised in Tyler, Texas, and ran all over the Astrodome field in the Texas high school football playoffs. For his next act, he ran all over the Southwest Conference for the Texas Longhorns and won the 1977 Heisman Award.

You had a real Texas superstar running back playing for a real Texas cowboy coach at a time when wearing a Stetson hat and boots became stylish nationwide.

The city of Houston went crazy for the Oilers.

Winning teams almost always gain popularity. Ticket sales would still have likely increased as the Oilers got closer and closer to the dream. The fact that you had true Texans like Bum Phillips and Earl Campbell as the faces of the team – that put Luv Ya Blue over the top.

Luv Ya Blue had a homecoming with 50,000 people after losing the AFC Championship Game. Luv Ya Blue had people shaking Bum Phillips' hand at the airport and saying hello as if he's just another Houston resident.

Other than the NFL job description, Bum was in many ways just like other Houstonians. He shared their values. He spoke Texas, breathed Texas, lived Texas.

What if, for example, Chuck Knox coached the Oilers and John Riggins was the star running back? Sure, the Oilers would see more fans in the Astrodome if they won, but would it have been the same? Would you see Robert Brazile, J.C. Wilson, and Mike Barber wearing western gear for their *Monday Night Football* profile pictures? Would any other coach say, "Dallas might be America's Team, but we're Texas' team?"

At quarterback, you had Dan Pastorini. He wasn't from Texas but it seemed like he could be. He understood and appreciated Texas and the Texan lifestyle. He made Texas his home.

He dated Farrah Fawcett, a television starlet from Corpus Christi whose iconic poster sold over 3 million copies in the mid-1970s. Pastorini also had movie star looks and appeared in a couple of films. He raced dragsters and boats when he wasn't playing football. He was a celebrity in circles outside of football.

Houston's oil-based economy also boomed. People from all over the country moved to Houston for employment. The *Houston Chronicle* sold papers across the nation to people scraping the want-ads.

The Luv Ya Blue sensation hasn't been duplicated by any American city or team. It likely can't be replicated. The number of variables that contributed to the phenomenon are too diverse and impossible to control.

You had a cowboy coach just as cowboy fashion became en vogue nationally. You had a homegrown, certified NFL legend in his prime. You had a celebrity quarterback dating a supermodel after he broke up with a Playboy centerfold model.

You had a winning team on the rise, a growing municipality on the upswing, and a groundswell of love and pride in city and team. That was the Houston Oilers of the late 1970s. That was Luv Ya Blue.

You can't recreate those times, those people, and those scenarios in a marketing meeting. Everything just came together at a certain moment in time, in a city ripe to embrace it.

Fans rallied, shouted, and danced as "Houston Oilers Number One" blared out of the Astrodome speakers. The song also played on radios and jukeboxes across Luv Ya Blue Nation.

A man named Lee Ofman wrote the song. Ofman grew up in Galveston. He moved to Austin to attend the University of Texas.

He joined a fraternity at UT. When one joins a fraternity, the person has what's called a big brother. The big brother is a person who helps orientate the new pledge into the fraternity and college life. Ofman's big brother was none other than Kinky Friedman.

Ofman graduated from UT and moved to Houston to find a job. He played music to make some money on the side. Finding a permanent job proved difficult, so he enrolled in South Texas School of Law and continued playing and singing.

A man named Sam Cammarata heard Ofman and wanted to manage him. Cammarata previously worked for boxing legend Rocky Marciano and now promoted musical acts.

Ofman and his acoustic guitar traveled across the country. He even got to meet Elvis and Ray Charles. Ofman eventually landed a long-standing gig at a bar in Houma, Louisiana.

This was in the early 1970s. The Miami Dolphins were winning, and both Ofman and bar owner Roy Brianne liked the Dolphins. Brianne said, "You know, you should write a song about the Dolphins."

Later that night, Ofman went home. The song all came out at once, "Miami Dolphins Number 1."

He played it for Brianne. Brianne loved it and financed a recording. Ofman recorded it in New Orleans. A Nashville-based promoter was hired to promote the record in Miami, just before the Dolphins hit the midway point in their undefeated 1972 season.

The promoter returned word saying, "You're a day late and a dollar short. There are a bunch of Dolphins songs out there."

Ofman was disappointed, but accepted the "day late, dollar short" as part of the music business. He still had his steady gig playing in Houma, Louisiana.

After Miami won Super Bowl 7, Lee and bar owner Roy Brianne watched television in the back of the bar. News footage showed the Dolphins returning to the airport after winning the Super Bowl. To Ofman's amazement, the fans sang, "Miami Dolphins Number 1."

Brianne asked, "Isn't that your song? If we're a day late and a dollar short, why are all these people signing it?"

Ofman called a friend who lived in Miami. Ofman asked, "Have you heard a song called, 'Miami Dolphins Number One?'"

His friend said that it got played so much that he might break his radio if he heard it one more time.

Ofman told him that he wrote the song.

His friend didn't believe him.

Ofman got booked some nice gigs around Miami beach. At some point, the Dolphins started playing the song at home games. Ofman hoped to secure a contract with the Dolphins, but the team said they weren't in the music business.

Ofman moved back to Houston. He scored gigs at some pretty nice clubs. One of the club owners knew about "Miami Dolphins Number 1" and said, "Hey, you know the Oilers are starting to win."

Ofman, still hurting from the experience from the Dolphins, said, "I don't want to write another fight song and go through all that again."

The club owner said, "You don't have to write a whole new song. Use the one you've got."

Ofman thought about it some more. He decided to make a demo with his band. One member surprised him by bringing a tuba to the session. They recorded the song on very modest equipment, a 3M Wollensak recorder. He added a few extra lyrics.

He drove down to the Oiler offices. The receptionist told him to leave the song and somebody would listen to it. He also had to leave the 3M Wollensak machine so they could play the recording.

Ofman next heard the song on television during a game. He was shocked. He wanted to re-record it because it was just a demo. He thought it could sound a lot better recorded with higher grade equipment. In the end, the recording became popular just the way it was.

Just like in Miami, Ofman obtained some nice gigs around the Houston area as a result. He soon moved to Nashville to follow his musical career. He even had a song placed in a Clint Eastwood movie.

"Houston Oilers Number One" gained a lot of attention and is the version that fans around the country seem to most recognize. Many outside of Florida are surprised to hear the Dolphins version.

The Dolphins still play the song at home games. The team occasionally invites Ofman to games. He has gotten to mingle with many of the Dolphins legends.

Lee Ofman didn't expect any of these things to happen. He also didn't record two versions of the song to create controversy. The two versions both just sort of happened. One person suggested he write a song about the Dolphins. Another suggested he redo the song for the Oilers. Both versions took on lives of their own and many more people know the song than know who wrote and sang it.

Lee is a big sports fan. He also loves music. He never thought the two paths would cross. He feels fortunate that fans just like him celebrated touchdowns and wins while his music floated through the stadium speakers.

The Oilers promotion department did their part to elevate the hysteria surrounding the team.

Monday Night Football was a huge deal in the 1970s. Only three major television networks existed at the time. Fans cherished the limited amount of NFL action available. *Sunday Night Football* and *Thursday Night Football* were years away. No ESPN. No Sunday Ticket. *Monday Night Football* was an enormous regular season showcase.

In 1978, the Oilers played at home against Miami on *Monday Night Football*. The Oilers staged a special promotion and everybody in the stadium had pom-poms. Nobody saw anything like it. The scene blew viewers' minds. ABC announcer Howard Cosell seemed overwhelmed by the spectacle. A banner in the stands said, "Look out America, Here Comes Houston."

Houston's promotion department invented a new idea for the upcoming Monday night game against the Steelers. Fans would receive a Luv Ya Blue sign to hold and wave to the beat of "Houston Oilers Number One." Like the 1978 game against Miami, the sign giveaway created a memorable display of support.

In recent times, some current pro and college teams have tried to have all fans wear the same color shirt for big games. Pro and college teams have given sections colored signs to spell out a message.

None of those scenes touch the fervor and excitement created by Houston fans during the Luv Ya Blue era.

CHAPTER 19

Week 15 – HOME VS. PITTSBURGH

NFL legend Frank Gifford anchored the *Monday Night Football* broadcasting team. The camera panned across the frenzied crowd at the Astrodome. Gifford remarked that Houston was more fired up than any city he could recall.

The trademark pom-poms bobbed. The new Luv Ya Blue signs rocked back and forth. The ecstatic crowd lifted the decibel meter into the red even before the kickoff of Houston's showdown with Pittsburgh.

Billy "White Shoes" Johnson stood on the sidelines in street clothes. He was on crutches and wore a special shoe. His presence let his teammates know that he wasn't backing down from his injury. He wanted to be there. He wasn't going to quit and being there subtly told his teammates not to quit.

Billy's story also said a lot about Bum Phillips. Billy suffered a devastating knee injury that caused him to miss most of 1978. Another injury sidelined him through almost all of 1979.

Most coaches released players that missed two seasons. Most coaches didn't want a guy taking up a roster spot while he rehabbed for two years. Bum Phillips wasn't like most coaches.

Phillips didn't quit on Billy Johnson, and Billy later recovered and continued his brilliant NFL career.

The biggest American news story of the time was the Iran Hostage Crisis. Iranian students took over 60 Americans hostage at the American Embassy in Tehran on November 4, 1979. Most hostages stayed in captivity for over a year. Twelve hostages, however, were released in late November of 1979.

Marine Sargent David Walker was one of the released hostages. He was on hand and honored before the game. There was a moment of silence and prayer for the remaining hostages during a moving ceremony before kickoff.

The Oilers would have owned a chance to win the division with a win over the Steelers had they defeated Cleveland the previous week. Instead, the Steelers now had a chance to win the division outright. A Pittsburgh win would seal the deal.

Houston kicked off to start the game. The Steelers fumbled but recovered 4 yards downfield. It was their longest gain of the opening drive. Houston's defense held Pittsburgh to a three-and-out.

Houston took over at their own 10.

An injury to right tackle Mo Townes shifted the offensive line. The versatile Conway Hayman switched to right tackle and David Carter started at left guard alongside Leon Gray.

Earl Campbell kept running. He took the ball on the first three plays and picked up a first down. He later earned another first down on third-and-2, despite seven Steelers lined up on the line of scrimmage. The Oilers established their running game early.

Pastorini called a play-action pass. Cornerback Ron Johnson had single coverage on Ken Burrough, a great matchup for the Oilers.

Burrough got a step ahead and Pastorini made a good throw. Johnson closed in at the last second and knocked the ball away.

On third-and-9, the Steelers double covered the Oiler receivers. Strong safety Donnie Shell covered tight end Mike Barber one-on-one. Pastorini spotted the single coverage and Barber got open. A good throw and a strong run gave the Oilers a first down on the Steeler 44.

On the next third down, the Oilers tried the same play, but a dropped ball forced a punt.

Although the Steelers stopped the Oilers on the drive, a few things happened in Houston's favor. They established the running game. They proved they could protect the quarterback and recognize single coverage.

The worst part for Pittsburgh was that they lost Hall of Fame linebacker Jack Ham for the game and ultimately for the season. Coach Chuck Noll and crew needed to replace a crucial piece of the Steel Curtain defense.

Houston put great pressure on Terry Bradshaw on first down. Bradshaw still found a way to complete a long pass to tight end Bennie Cunningham. Houston later forced a third down, but Bradshaw's low pass to Lynn Swann allowed the receiver to slide and catch it for another first down.

Again, football is a game of inches. Pastorini and Burrough missed a long gain by inches. Bradshaw missed getting sacked by inches and completed a long pass. Swann caught a ball inches away from the turf for another first down.

The Steelers soon faced fourth-and-inches on the Oiler 25. Chuck Noll believed short-yardage plays could determine the game. He decided to forgo the field goal attempt and go for the first down.

The tide of inches turned Houston's way. Bradshaw handed off to Rocky Bleier. Bleier ran to the right side. Andy Dorris shed his blocker and made a strong tackle to stop Bleier short of the first down.

The Astrodome crowd went berserk.

Dorris still remembers the play. "We were in a goal-line type prevent, which means you just dig in on the defensive line. I was able to defeat the blocks and throw them away. It happened so quickly that when I got rid of the block, (Bleier) and I just ran into each other. It was just a split second, it happened so quickly.

"He had a running start and I was flat-footed at that point. I was able to stay up and I guess that's where that strength comes from. When you're standing still in that split second, what you do in that time frame, that's where your strength comes from. When you're moving, it's different because you have that inertia working for you, you have leverage."

Dorris credits his off-season conditioning program for the extra strength to stop Bleier after Bleier had a running start.

An action-packed first quarter produced zero points. The Oilers missed a field goal early in the second quarter, but the game's momentum stayed with Houston thanks to two events.

The game was a scoreless tie early in the second quarter of the much-anticipated game.

The Steelers started a drive on their own 27. A 5-yard penalty painted the Steelers into a likely passing situation.

Elvin Bethea charged off the snap. He ran inside and forced Bradshaw out of the pocket. Bradshaw rushed a throw.

Linebacker Art Stringer intercepted the ball and ran it back to the 22. Stringer had just returned to the lineup after missing several games due to an injury. His interception tallied 33 for the Oilers that season.

A first down on the 22-yard line often means easy points, especially at home. The Steel Curtain defense, however, rarely allowed easy points. Defensive tackle Joe Greene looked like he lined up in the backfield on first down and stopped Earl Campbell for no gain.

The play was typical Joe Greene. 1979 marked the tenth consecutive year that the Temple, Texas native made the Pro Bowl. He seemed to always place himself in the wrong place at the wrong time for opposing offenses. He launched through the line like a thunderbolt.

The Oilers contained Joe Greene on second down. Linebacker Jack Lambert clogged the middle instead. Lambert stuffed the run to make it third-and-long.

Those two plays illustrated one major problem with beating the Steelers. Superstars and future Hall of Famers lined up all over the field. If you were lucky enough to get past Joe Greene, Jack Lambert rewarded you with your next challenge. You still needed to block L.C. Greenwood, too.

The defense is allowed 11 players for each play. Six Steeler defenders made the Pro Bowl in 1979. You don't need to be a math major to know that's more than half.

The Steeler defense multiplied trouble. They not only shut offenses down with solid play, they forced good players into making mental errors. That explains why on third-and-long the Oilers committed both a clipping penalty and a holding penalty. The clipping foul sent Houston back to the Steeler 35 with a third-and-20, nearly out of field goal range. At that point, you just hope the Steelers somehow make a mistake.

Sometimes you get lucky. Especially at home.

In this case, Steeler cornerback Ron Johnson bumped Mike Renfro while a Pastorini pass headed Renfro's way. The pass interference penalty gave Houston a second chance with a first down at Pittsburgh's 17.

The Steelers lined up seven men at the line of scrimmage with Jack Lambert centered close behind, hoping to stop Campbell. They had lined up that way often so far this game.

Houston staged a good counter call, an inside handoff to Tim Wilson, who quickly cut to his right. The entire Steeler defense headed the opposite direction.

Linebacker Dennis "Dirt" Winston proved agile enough to twist his body against his momentum. Winston fell but made enough contact with Wilson that Joe Greene had time to get back into position and make the tackle.

Another case of inches. Had Wilson been a few more inches away from Winston, he might have scored. Instead, he only picked up 3 yards.

Campbell took the next play to his left. Mel Blount burst through the line and tackled Campbell for a loss. Another Pro Bowler. Another future Hall of Famer. Another third-and-long, followed by another Steeler stop.

Houston lined up for a field goal. The formation was a ruse. Gifford Nielsen took the snap, but instead of placing it down for Toni Fritsch to kick, he attempted to flip the ball to Ted Thompson.

The ball fell from Thompson's hands. Officials ruled the play an incomplete pass.

Despite the missed scoring opportunity, Gregg Bingham pointed out that there was still benefit in calling the fake field goal. The Oilers knew they'd likely make the playoffs no matter what. The fake field goal forced future opponents to waste valuable practice time preparing for the possibility. That reduced the time teams used preparing for plays the Oilers would actually run. Bingham called such plays, "time wasters."

For right now, however, the Oilers struck out on this at bat. A first down on the Steeler 22 and a second chance on the Steeler 17 netted zero points.

Houston's defense made sure the Steelers also struck out. They forced another three-and-out. The Oilers started the next drive at the 50.

So far, Houston had won the field position game but had no points to show for it. The trend continued. The game stayed a defensive war and both defenses recorded sacks and near interceptions as the two teams traded punts deep into the second quarter.

The Steelers often started drives inside their own 20. They started on their own 14 late in the second quarter. Bradshaw fired to tight end Randy Grossman on third-and-7, right after the two-minute warning. The play took Pittsburgh all the way to the Houston 35.

Bradshaw liked that play so much that he ran it again.

Robert Brazile read the play perfectly. He intercepted the pass and ran hard. He looked to the sideline but couldn't quite get there. He gained considerable yardage in the center of the field.

He put his head down as two Steelers approached. He took a helmet-to-helmet collision from both players and was down for a considerable amount of time. Thankfully, he eventually jumped up and ran to the sidelines under his own power.

Brazile's return gave Houston the ball at Pittsburgh's 25-yard line. Hall of Fame quarterback Fran Tarkenton, part of the *Monday Night Football* broadcast team, stated that he would choose to throw the ball on first down in that situation.

As if on cue, Pastorini took the snap and dropped back to pass. He zipped the ball to Burrough through a window between two defenders. Burrough wrapped his hands around the ball for a touchdown. The Astrodome crowd exploded into cheers.

Houston took a 7-0 lead into the locker room at halftime.

The Oilers shut out the NFL's top-ranked offense for one half. The defense halted a Steeler running attack that garnered 380 yards against Cleveland. Pittsburgh held a mere 21 rushing yards to their credit in the Astrodome.

Conversely, the Oilers established a running game with 70 rushing yards in the first half.

Pittsburgh started the second half in good field position after a short Oiler punt. They kicked a field goal, making it 7-3. It was Houston's turn to respond.

A play-action pass to Rich Caster on first down gained over 20 yards. Passes to Carpenter and Renfro balanced with Earl Campbell's runs, and moved Houston to Pittsburgh's 15-yard line. Houston soon faced third-and-inches at the Steeler 5.

Earl Campbell got the ball. Joe Greene crashed through the line. Campbell ran right and avoided Greene, but Dennis "Dirt" Winston tackled Campbell.

The Oilers played conservative and kicked a field goal. Houston led, 10-3.

Pittsburgh avoided a Houston touchdown, but important things happened for the Oilers on that possession. Their offense effectively ran and passed against the Steelers. Houston established a balanced offense for the second half. Most importantly, the Oilers scored and extended their lead.

The ensuing possession meant a lot. Pittsburgh could tie the game. The Oilers could shut Pittsburgh down and give their offense a chance to go up by two scores.

The Steelers usually prevailed in such circumstances. Often in strange ways.

Larry Anderson returned the kickoff to the Steeler 41. Franco Harris, silent until now, took a screen pass to the Oiler 47. On third-and-3, Harris got a first down inside the 33.

An odd twist followed.

Bradshaw dropped back to throw. Linebacker Ted Washington busted through and chased Bradshaw backward. Washington grabbed Bradshaw's left arm near the 45-yard line and pushed Bradshaw further back. He grabbed Bradshaw's hip and started to toss Bradshaw to the turf.

Bradshaw desperately tossed the ball. The ill-advised pass floated downfield, up for grabs. The ball bounced off receiver John Stallworth and directly into the hands of Lynn Swann at Houston's 13-yard line.

The mix of executing good plays combined with peculiar strokes of luck characterized many Steeler wins. Pittsburgh made very few mistakes as a team. Steeler head coach Chuck Noll made sure of that with rigorous preparation.

The Immaculate Reception is the most famous example of bizarre bounces that seemed to bound toward Pittsburgh more often than not. Some games it seemed like teams played against both the Steelers and Lady Luck. Luck didn't always go Pittsburgh's way, of course, but the Steelers won so often that it magnified times when an up-for-grabs pass to avoid a sack bounced off one Hall of Famer's hands into the waiting arms of another Hall of Famer for a 20-yard gain.

Two plays later, Bradshaw hit Swann for an easy touchdown. Or so it seemed. Like I said, luck didn't always go the Steelers way and no team plays perfect football.

A holding call nullified the touchdown. Afterward, excellent coverage forced two straight incompletions.

The Steelers lined up for a field goal. The usually reliable Matt Bahr missed to the right.

The freaky pass play turned out to be innocuous. Indeed, the result of the drive energized the crowd even more and frustrated the Steelers who came away with nothing.

Houston's offense capitalized on their chance. Another well-balanced drive moved Houston into Pittsburgh territory as the game marched into the fourth quarter.

Toni Fritsch kicked a field goal and extended Houston's lead to 13-3. Pittsburgh needed two scores to win or tie. Eleven minutes remained in the game.

The Oilers knew the Steelers needed to pass. They brought their pass rush.

On a third-and-3 play, Bradshaw escaped and ran up the middle for 20 yards to the Oiler 43. Franco Harris took a pitchout on the next play and blazed all the way to the Oiler 9.

Seven minutes remained.

Bradshaw handed off to Rocky Bleier. Bleier handed off to Lynn Swann on a reverse. Swann evaded two tacklers with a piercing cut to the inside. He darted toward the end zone and dove through a tiny slice of space between three tacklers. The referees signaled touchdown.

The extra point made it 13-10 with 6:46 left.

The sequence underlined the difficulty of defending Pittsburgh's offense, especially when the game hung in the balance. Bradshaw made a huge play on third down. Then, Franco Harris made a play. Then, Lynn Swann scored on what in today's world would be the *SportsCenter* "Play of the Day."

Three Hall of Famers. Three big plays. And a serious cut into Houston's lead.

Four players on the Steelers' offense made the Pro Bowl that year. Swann didn't make the Pro Bowl that year but remained an

All-Pro level threat. Pittsburgh fielded several legendary players on both sides of the ball.

The Oilers needed to answer with points and a time-consuming drive. A field goal would force Pittsburgh to score a touchdown. An Oiler touchdown might clinch the game.

Houston started on their own 30 and quickly reminded Pittsburgh that great players played for both teams. Earl Campbell broke through Jack Lambert's tackle and raced all the way to the Steeler 35. Rich Caster, Mike Barber and Tim Wilson teamed up for important blocks, and Campbell's speed made it an exceptional play.

Tim Wilson ran a trap play for 8 yards. Pastorini milked the clock. Time slipped under five minutes.

Earl Campbell went over 100 yards for the game. The Steelers hadn't given up 100 yards to a running back since the middle of the previous season.

Pastorini literally stood at the line before the play and watched the clock tick. The game clock slipped under three minutes. When the play clock neared zero, Pastorini handed off to Rob Carpenter. Carpenter got inside the Steeler 20.

A facemask penalty against the Steelers put Houston at Pittsburgh's 8-yard line. Just over two minutes remained in the game. The crowd smelled victory and loudly rejoiced. An offside penalty made it first-and-goal at the 4.

Pastorini called for an end run left to Carpenter. Carpenter took off with the ball. Defensive back J.T. Thomas had an angle to make the stop and closed in toward Carpenter.

Thomas met the ground instead, as Earl Campbell leveled Thomas with a superb block.

Carpenter crossed the goal line. Touchdown, Oilers. The roof nearly lifted off the Astrodome.

The Oilers led, 20-10. The drive erased over four and a half minutes of game clock. Such a drive squashed the hopes of most teams. In fact, the *Monday Night Football* announcing crew pretty much ceded the game to the Oilers. Chuck Noll wasn't tuned in to their broadcast.

The Oiler pass rush hurried Bradshaw, but he still completed a pass across midfield. Franco Harris took a pass to the Oiler 34 with just over 90 seconds left. Bradshaw chucked a pass to an open John Stallworth for a touchdown.

Bradshaw. Harris. Stallworth. Three plays. Three Hall of Famers. Another touchdown.

The 3-play, 71-yard drive took about 40 seconds. Pittsburgh had 1:20 left and all three timeouts. The tenacious Steelers needed only an onside kick and a field goal to tie a game that many believed was over less than a minute ago.

A 5-yard penalty against Houston set the kickoff at the Pittsburgh 40. Should Pittsburgh recover, they'd be that much closer to a game-tying field goal. Pittsburgh lined up for the onside kick.

Steeler kicker Matt Bahr nudged the onside kick to the right side. His teammate Larry Anderson caught it in stride. He stepped out of bounds around the Houston 45. The Oilers didn't even get close to fielding the ball. The play possibly marked the first paragraph in a crushing chapter.

Chaos abounded. Uncertainty surrounded the play. Anderson sprinted back toward midfield, pointing at the ground and yelling.

Players gathered at the 50-yard line. The officials huddled up. The side judge, who was right in front of the play, said the ball didn't travel the necessary 10 yards before Anderson touched it. The referee announced the call to the crowd and assessed an illegal touching penalty against Pittsburgh. The Steelers got to rekick.

Replays showed the ball likely broke the plane of the 50-yard line before Anderson grabbed it. Anderson stepped in front of the side judge, however, and that may have blocked the side judge's view of the play. Today's instant replay might have overruled the call. Replays didn't matter in 1979. The Oilers received a second chance on the onside kick.

Mike Barber helped them take advantage of the second chance and recovered the second attempt. Again, the game seemed over.

The Steelers still had three timeouts, however. The defense stopped Houston on three plays and Pittsburgh called timeout as quickly as the whistle blew.

Cliff Parsley made a nice punt for the Oilers. The kick pinned the Steelers back at their own 9 with about 40 seconds left. Houston needed to stop Pittsburgh from duplicating their previous 40-second drive.

Franco Harris got wide open in the flat on first down. He had a running start and lots of open Astroturf in front of him.

Bradshaw tossed Harris the ball. Harris dropped it. He bowed his head in disappointment. Oiler fans breathed a collective sigh. Thirty-four seconds remained.

Rocky Bleier got open on second down. Bradshaw fired him the ball, and he also dropped it. Twenty-eight seconds remained.

Bradshaw looked deep on third down. The Steelers desperately needed a play. Vernon Perry made one for the Oilers instead. He batted down a long pass.

The Steelers were down to their last play. Twenty-two seconds remained.

Bradshaw took the snap. He dropped straight back. The Oiler secondary blanketed the Steeler receivers. The Oiler pass rush closed in on Bradshaw. Defensive end Jessie Baker slammed Bradshaw to the turf.

Pom-poms and Luv Ya Blue signs waved. The Astrodome rocked and celebrated Houston's 20-17 win.

The Oilers entered the final week of the 1979 season in a first-place tie with the Steelers for the AFC Central title. At worst, the Oilers would host a wildcard game in the AFC playoffs.

One beautiful thing about 1970s football was the homemade banners that decked the rails of NFL stadiums. Fans spray painted slogans on bedsheets or made signs out of cardboard or poster board. Some were fancy, some were artistic, others quite crude.

Monday Night Football broadcasts inspired even more signs than usual. Oiler fans welcomed ABC and the broadcast crew of Frank Gifford, Fran Tarkenton, and Howard Cosell. Many signs listed the name of a town from which people traveled to see the game, saying things like, "Baytown, Texas loves the Oilers." Others showed support for individual players stating, "Pastorini for President" and "God Bless Mama Campbell."

One banner pasted in a corner of the Astrodome painted a million pictures. The words captured what the 1979 Houston Oilers and their fans felt in their hearts after the Oilers won 5 of 6 games over some of the NFL's toughest opponents to guarantee a place in the playoffs.

The banner held only two simple words.

"We Believe."

CHAPTER 20
Week 16 – HOME VS. PHILADELPHIA

By beating Pittsburgh, the Oilers accomplished two important tasks toward the dream of winning Super Bowl 14. The team reminded Pittsburgh that they could beat the Steelers after losing the last two head-to-head matchups by a total of 60 points.

Houston also clinched a playoff berth. Only five AFC teams made the playoffs, and one of those teams would represent the AFC in Super Bowl 14 at Pasadena, California. You can't win the Super Bowl if you don't make the playoffs.

Local and national sports media discussed the Steelers onside kick call during the week. The game scored the second-highest *Monday Night Football* ratings in history at the time, earning a 40 percent share of viewers. A lot of people saw the onside kick and everybody had an opinion about the call.

Art McNally, the NFL's head of officials, issued a statement which said the officials incorrectly called a penalty and that the Steelers legally recovered the original onside kick. Interestingly, the league added that although the side judge made the call, the line judge didn't fully understand onside kick rules. He thought the ball needed to touch an opposing player or the ground after traveling 10 yards to be recovered by the kicking team.

The topic of using video replays to confirm or correct calls during games wasn't discussed, although game footage inspired the NFL to prepare a statement.

Neither the Steelers nor Oilers publicly stated that the onside kick decided the game. Chuck Noll simply noted that the ball went 10 yards. Bum Phillips listed a few questionable calls that went the Steelers way.

Although the Steelers weren't happy with the onside kick ruling, they complimented the Oilers on their victory. Noll said it was the best game he'd ever seen the Oilers play. Lynn Swann agreed. The local media called the win one of the finest games in Oiler history.

The Oilers beat the Super Bowl champs on *Monday Night Football*. A few days before, they beat NFC Champion Dallas on Thanksgiving. The national audience recognized that Houston belonged in the same sentence with championship teams.

The Houston media touted the Oilers and expressed both excitement and hope for the upcoming playoffs. Joy over the wins and the fans' hysteria replaced criticism in newspaper columns. Writers now applauded Pastorini. Bum Phillips heard only praise-inspired questions. The Oiler derrick started peaking at precisely the right time.

The Eagles and Oilers entered their Week 16 matchup with playoff tickets already punched.

Philadelphia owned a 10-5 record, knotted with Dallas and Washington for first place in the NFC East. Playoff brackets already carved Philadelphia's name into a wildcard slot. The winner of Week 16's Washington at Dallas affair determined the division champion.

The Eagles hoped for a Washington loss and a chance at a home playoff game.

The Oilers sat at 11-4, tied for the best mark in the National Football League. Unfortunately, one of the other two 11-4 teams was a division rival.

The Oilers only chance to obtain the AFC Central Division crown rested inside the unsteady hands of the Buffalo Bills. The Bills needed to win at Pittsburgh for Houston to win the division. Houston sported a better conference record than the Steelers, so if the Bills found a way to win, then the Oilers would claim the division championship regardless of the outcome of their game against Philadelphia.

The Steelers claimed a tiebreaker over the Oilers if both teams won and finished 12-4. Pittsburgh held a substantial margin in point-differential against division rivals, largely thanks to the Oilers' Week 2 loss at Pittsburgh.

The fact that the Oilers still possessed a chance to win the division speaks for how great of a team the 1979 Oilers proved to be. If both Pittsburgh and Houston finished 11-5, Houston won the division via a high-tier tiebreaker: conference records. If both teams finished 12-4, the Steelers won by virtue of the fifth tiebreaker, net points in division matchups. Pittsburgh and Houston stood that close to each other going into the NFL's final week.

The Bills hadn't found a way to defeat a playoff-bound opponent all year. They weren't about to start winning in Pittsburgh's Three Rivers Stadium. In fact, the Bills failed to score. Pittsburgh walked off the field with a 28-0 win and clinched the AFC Central Division title before the Oilers-Eagles matchup kicked off in the late afternoon.

The Oilers earned a home wildcard game whether they finished 12-4 or 11-5. The game meant nothing to Houston in terms of standings.

Earl Campbell needed 2 rushing touchdowns to break the NFL's single-season rushing touchdown record. He needed about 50 rushing yards to top both Walter Payton and Cardinal rookie Ottis Anderson for the NFL's rushing title.

Campbell took care of statistical business early. He scored a second-quarter touchdown to tie the all-time single-season mark. He bolted for 134 yards on only 16 carries and pinned down the league rushing title. He crossed the 100-yard benchmark for the seventh consecutive game, only the second back in history to accomplish that feat.

He then went into the locker room for halftime. He rested for the second half.

The Oilers also rested Dan Pastorini in the fourth quarter, placing Gifford Nielsen in charge. Bum Phillips wanted his players ready for the playoffs and sought to avoid injuries during a game that didn't matter in the standings.

The Oilers lost the game, 26-20, but already looked ahead to the next step of the dream.

Houston found out their playoff opponent on Monday night. Denver and San Diego met to determine the AFC West champion, the loser sliding into the wildcard round at Houston.

The Chargers produced a 17-7 win at home. San Diego quarterback Dan Fouts broke Joe Namath's single-season passing record with 4,082 yards on the year.

The Chargers finished 12-4, tied with Pittsburgh for the NFL's best record. Houston's 11-5 record matched them with Dallas and Philadelphia in the win column for the next-highest total.

Those records lost their meaning after playoff seeding. Houston needed to climb an extra mile against opponents who dreamt the same dream and believed in all the possibilities the 1979 NFL playoffs presented.

The regular season provided magical moments and landmark franchise victories. All came together to weave a story of team, tenacity, and family. The entire city of Houston rallied around the red, white, and Columbia blue, perhaps more than any other city has rallied around any other team. The wins against Dallas and Pittsburgh, as well as the exceptional running of Earl Campbell, are memories shared at sports bars and family gatherings to this day.

The 1979 Houston Oilers won most of the games against teams they should have beaten. The team dug deeper and pulled out wins against elite teams. Houston topped the teams that won the previous eight Super Bowls -- Pittsburgh, Dallas, Miami, and Oakland.

The chips fell where they may, and enough went Houston's way to earn a home wildcard game. Now it was time to find out if the Oilers had enough chips to make it all the way to Pasadena, California, and Super Bowl 14.

PART 5
THE EXTRA MILE: THE PLAYOFFS

Twenty-eight teams started with a dream. Ten remained. Several good teams like the New England Patriots, Washington Redskins, and Oakland Raiders woke up short of the playoffs.

Washington's season ended in historic and nightmarish fashion in Dallas. The Redskins led 34-21 in the fourth quarter, ready to cruise into the NFL playoffs. Time ticked and tocked away, down to under three minutes. The game appeared over.

Roger Staubach had other ideas. He put on his Captain Comeback suit and tossed two touchdowns in the game's final two minutes to win, 35-34. The win clinched the NFC East for the Cowboys. Washington became the first team in NFL history to finish 10-6 and miss the playoffs.

Five teams made the AFC playoffs. Houston faced two of those teams, Miami and Pittsburgh, in the regular season. Houston won their only matchup with Miami and split with the Steelers.

The Houston Oilers entered the playoffs believing as a team, as a family, and the Luv Ya Blue community believed as a city.

Bum Phillips and crew showed that 1978 wasn't a fluke, rather a preview of what this group could accomplish together. It was time for one of Phillips' favorite sayings, "Every man get a man. Every good man get two."

CHAPTER 21

Wildcard Round – HOME VS. DENVER

The Denver Broncos made the playoffs for the third consecutive season under head coach Red Miller. The Broncos won the AFC in 1977 and played in Super Bowl 12. The Broncos knew how to win playoff games before the Oilers even made the playoffs.

The experienced Broncos made a formidable opponent. Their Orange Crush defense featured a solid linebacking corps that included All-Pros Tom Jackson and Randy Gradishar. Quarterback Craig Morton led both Dallas and Denver to Super Bowls. He played college football at Cal, coached by future NFL legends Marv Levy as head coach and Bill Walsh as offensive coordinator.

The game was the first playoff in Astrodome history, and the Oilers first home playoff game since the 1962 American Football League Championship Game.

The rabid Oiler fan base could now finally be seen and heard in the NFL playoffs. The Luv Ya Blue pom-poms and signage bobbed their way into the postseason with a thunderous cheer.

Even Santa got fired up for the game played on December 23. He walked around the field giving treats to fans with his hair dyed Columbia blue. He appeared in both the Christmas spirit and the Oiler spirit.

NFL players don't need extra incentive to win playoff games, but Curley Culp always felt a double dose of motivation against Denver. The Broncos drafted him in the second round in 1968 but traded him to Kansas City. Since then, Culp always circled the Broncos on the schedule. Now, the game meant even more in the playoffs.

The Oilers and the city were like family. Appropriately, Robert Brazile's parents attended the wildcard game at the Astrodome in celebration of their wedding anniversary. He appreciated the way the Oilers organization made sure that his parents enjoyed themselves, and Robert wanted to play an extra good game for his family.

Defensive end Andy Dorris owned another personal rivalry in this game. Denver tackle Claudie Minor got the best of Dorris in previous matchups, and Dorris wanted a little payback.

Team. Family. Personal challenge. All of these presented themselves as additional inspiration for the Houston Oilers as they rushed out of the tunnel to an exuberant crowd.

The Oilers won the toss and elected to receive. The crowd cheered so loud as the Oilers took the field that the television announcers raised their voices to be heard.

The crowd tempered itself for the offense to hear Pastroini call signals, but loud cheers resumed once plays started. Like a flammable liquid, the Oiler fans waited to explode.

Earl Campbell and Tim Wilson paved the Oilers' path with solid runs to pick up first downs. Houston earned another first down on a pass interference penalty.

On third-and-9, Ronnie Coleman dashed out of the backfield on a long pass route down the middle. He got several steps ahead of the

Denver defense and Pastorini launched the ball. The throw was a bit long, but Coleman dove fully outstretched to reel in a spectacular 41-yard catch.

The crowd erupted. The Oilers knocked on the door at Denver's 14 yard-line.

The drive resulted in a field goal. The crowd's enthusiasm soared. Scoring points on the first possession was important to keep the fans' momentum strong.

Denver started at their own 20. Craig Morton hit the Broncos' offensive ignition switch. He suffered from a pulled stomach muscle but knew how to win playoff games.

Morton called high percentage plays to grind out first downs and eat up clock. The more time Earl Campbell sat on the bench, the better from a Broncos' perspective. Morton mixed runs with short passes, often throwing to his running backs.

Morton called a play-action pass from midfield on a second-and-7. He tossed to halfback Otis Armstrong. Armstrong picked up the first down and ran out of bounds.

Oiler safety Vernon Perry couldn't stop his own momentum and banged into Armstrong near the Bronco bench. Denver defensive end Barney Chavous jumped off the bench and charged Perry. Perry grabbed a nearby official to shield himself. The full officiating crew rushed over to halt the skirmish.

Offsetting personal foul penalties ensued. The Bronco drive continued inside the Oiler 40.

Morton extended his success mixing runs with play-action passes to tight ends and running backs. Denver got to the Oiler 3 on a short flare to running back Dave Preston.

Houston's defense clogged up the run near the goal line. They forced an incompletion with a safety blitz by Mike Reinfeldt. On third-and-goal from the 7, however, Morton hit Preston near the goal line. Preston dove underneath three defenders and slid into the end zone.

The Broncos led, 7-3.

The Oilers built a second drive as the first quarter expired. The Broncos' Orange Crush defense held tough, however. They limited Earl Campbell to almost 2 yards beneath his season average of 4.6 yards per carry.

The Broncos stopped the Oiler drive on a fourth-and-inches, and Denver took over at their own 45 as the second quarter began. They immediately crossed midfield on an Otis Armstrong run. Denver earned a first down and slowly grinded their way down field.

Craig Morton looked for a big play on the ensuing third down. He dropped back to pass. He slipped and moved to his right. Andy Dorris shoved Claudie Minor backward and sunk his grip into Morton. Morton went down.

The sack knocked the Broncos out of field goal range. That was an important win for Andy Dorris against Claudie Minor and a big stop for the Houston defense.

Pastorini came out aggressive. He threw deep to Kenny Burrough. Burrough leapt for the ball and sustained a hit from Denver defensive back Louis Wright. Burrough landed on his injured tailbone, and the ball fell incomplete. Burrough hobbled to the sidelines.

The Oilers hit two more setbacks. A false start made it second-and-15. The often sure-handed Mike Barber dropped a pass. That set up third-and-long.

Barber ran down the sideline and Pastorini threw to him again. Cornerback Louis Wright bore down on Barber and placed a big hit on the tight end just as the ball got there. This time, however, Barber held on for a 31-yard gain.

Campbell then made a solid gain on first down, helped by Barber's solid block. The Oilers ended up punting on the series, but key things happened, both positive and negative.

The negative, of course, was the loss of Ken Burrough. The tailbone injury he suffered against Dallas still hampered his agility and created a great deal of pain. His availability for the rest of the playoffs was in question, a large concern for the Oiler offense.

Two positive things happened to sway the narrative Houston's way. Mike Barber responded to missing one play by making two. His big third-down catch illustrated that the Oiler way was not to dwell on mistakes, but to move forward and make something happen. He made a key catch and then a key block to further the drive.

Secondly, field position favored Houston. The 31-yard catch, combined with an effective punt from Cliff Parsley, tacked the Broncos back to their own 11 to start the next series. Driving 89 yards against Houston's defense in the Astrodome appeared a remote possibility. If the Oiler defense forced a three-and-out, the offense would likely start their next drive with good field position.

The sequence played Houston's way. Robert Brazile and Gregg Bingham stopped the Broncos' third-down play. The Oilers got the ball back at Denver's 46.

A play-action pass to Tim Wilson gained 20 yards on the first play. Campbell broke three tackles to create a 5-yard gain out of a potential 6-yard loss. That Oiler way of moving forward through adversity put them on the Bronco 22.

Houston looked like they would either narrow Denver's lead to 7-6 with a field goal or take the lead with a touchdown.

A turnover stopped that possibility. Pastorini threw toward a slanting receiver and defensive back Bill Thompson stepped in front of the pass. A lost opportunity, but the sequence revealed how a couple of plays on a previous drive can lead to success on later drives.

The crowd seemed deflated after the interception, but Houston's defense played inspired football. The Oilers forced a three-and-out.

The Oilers' next drive started on their own 26. Not bad, but not the ideal starting point from which the previous drive started.

The first half's two-minute warning struck as Houston faced a third-and-6. The once effusive crowd quietly watched.

Pastorini shook off the recent interception and fired a completion to Rob Carpenter for the first down. Tom Jackson ushered a forearm club to Carpenter's helmet on the play, and the Oilers gained an extra 15 yards via penalty. The ball rested at the Bronco 42.

Houston found themselves near the starting point of the previous drive. Second chances don't come often, both in life and in the NFL playoffs.

A score late in the first half meant a lot in this game. Not only would the Oilers carry momentum and a possible lead into the locker room, but Houston could also prevent serious damage. Denver had a 7-3 lead and would receive the second half kickoff. If Houston failed to score and Denver scored a touchdown on their first possession of the second half, then Houston would trail by 11. Eleven points was an especially steep hill to climb in the playoffs.

Pastorini tossed a flare to Earl Campbell for 7 yards. Dan paid a heavy price, taking blows from two Denver linemen after the throw. He crawled to his feet and went to the sideline after calling timeout.

He shook off the cobwebs and walked to the huddle. The huddle also featured Ken Burrough again. Oiler grit and brotherhood dug in to press forward.

The crowd felt the toughness. An infectious chant of "Go, Go, Go" slowly built into a crescendo.

Pastorini took the snap and faked a handoff to Tim Wilson. Mike Barber came around for a reverse, but Pastorini also faked a handoff to him. Dan turned and lofted a pass to Wilson, who now was about 20 yards downfield. Wilson caught the ball and the crowd went nuts.

Houston called timeout. They were at Denver's 16 with 1:26 left in the half.

Two Earl Campbell runs into the Orange Crush defense earned the Oilers a first-and-goal on the 3.

The Oiler crowd grew almost as loud as at the start of the game. "Houston Oilers Number One" played during the timeout as a sea of pom-poms rocked like fist pumps at a rock concert.

The Broncos stopped the first-down play, but not the second-down play. Earl Campbell crossed the goal line for an Oiler touchdown. The crowd broke into a frenzy.

The players also broke into a frenzy, chasing the ball. Campbell dropped the ball shortly after breaking the goal line for a score. Players, including Campbell, couldn't tell if it was a touchdown in the middle of the action.

Several players scurried toward the back of the end zone to chase the ball. Campbell pulled a groin muscle in the pursuit. He lay injured in the end zone while the crowd cheered his touchdown.

The Astrodome soon turned quiet after the crowd noticed Earl was still down on the turf. He slowly rose to his feet and the crowd roared again.

The touchdown put the Oilers ahead 10-7 at the half, but the crucial score came at a cost. Earl Campbell wouldn't return to the field that day. The Oiler family needed to rally around each other and win without their superstar running back.

The Broncos started the second half with a play-action pass to Otis Armstrong for 9 yards. The game plan appeared the same as in the first half. The Broncos focused on short passes to running backs and tight ends. Denver mixed in some runs and hoped to slowly grind out yardage and time off the clock.

Denver got to midfield without any trouble.

Andy Dorris said, "Enough."

Morton faded back to throw. Dorris plowed through Claudie Minor and smothered Morton for his second sack of the day. Ted Washington assisted in the 7-yard loss.

Two plays later, Dorris wanted more. He shredded through Minor and crushed Morton again. Dorris notched his third sack of the day against his arch enemy, Claudie Minor.

The Bronco drive that started smoothly crumpled under the weight of Houston's pass rush. The aging Craig Morton, in his fifteenth NFL season, got up slower and slower as the Astrodome's crowd cheered louder and louder.

Momentum shook in Houston's favor. Games, especially playoff games, often have moments when everything starts to swing in one team's direction. This matchup's atmosphere showed signs of quickly blowing Houston's way.

The team needed to rise without Earl Campbell, however. Ken Burrough also missed the start of the second half.

Veteran Oiler backs Ronnie Coleman and Tim Wilson teamed up for a first down in Campbell's absence. Rob Carpenter rushed for 10 yards to the Oiler 40. The Oilers showed signs of taking control with a long, slow scoring drive.

Pastorini called a play-action pass. He faked the handoff and rolled to his right to evade linebacker Larry Evans. He then collapsed, untouched.

Pastorini lay on the ground writhing in pain. The training staff huddled around him. Pastroini stayed on the ground for a few minutes. He finally stood up with help. Robert Brazile and George Reihner carried Dan off the field, in a show of offensive and defensive brotherhood and solidarity in a time of need. Doctors determined Pastorini suffered a groin injury and couldn't return.

"All of a sudden, I felt this pop," Pastorini said. "People could hear it on the sideline and said it sounded like a gunshot. I mean, it was painful. I just went down like I was shot. I couldn't walk."

First, Burrough. Then, Campbell. Now, Pastorini. The three pillars of the Houston offense, sidelined.

Gifford Nielsen reported for Pastorini in a second-and-long situation. That became third-and-long, and soon fourth-and-long in punt formation.

Seven minutes remained in the third quarter. Houston's defense needed to make plays. The slim 3-point margin against a veteran quarterback who led two teams to Super Bowls seemed vulnerable.

Gregg Bingham reminded himself of how hard the team worked to get this far. He thought back to training camp. He thought about the pain of losing to Pittsburgh in '78.

Denver immediately picked up a first down, with a toss to running back Dave Preston. Running back Larry Canada gained another first down. Denver moved past their own 40 in two plays.

The injuries seemed to shift the momentum toward the Broncos.

The Houston defense stiffened quickly. The line stuffed a running play and Vernon Perry batted down two straight passes. Denver punted.

Gifford Nielsen handled the conservative offense well and took as much off the clock as possible. Even punter Cliff Parsley waited until the play clock's last seconds to call a snap. The third quarter expired as Houston clung to their 10-7 lead.

The Broncos started driving early in the fourth. Running plays by Armstrong and Preston placed Denver on the Houston 45.

The Oilers pushed back. Bingham laid a tough hit on running back Jim Jensen on a pass play. The blow temporarily knocked Jensen out of the game. Bingham wasn't there to back down. He was there to hit. He was there to play football. He was there to win.

The Oilers forced a punt, but trouble soon approached. Nielsen threw a play-action pass on first down. Randy Gradishar batted the ball up, and a volleyball game broke out in the open field. The ball bounced off two or three players without hitting the ground. Denver's Bob Swenson eventually came away with an interception.

Winning in the playoffs requires a lot of skill, tenacity, and muscle. It also requires a touch of luck. The Broncos touched some luck on that play.

Denver set up shop at Houston's 26, with a perfect opportunity to kick a game-tying field goal or move ahead with a touchdown.

Houston's defense stepped on the field with swagger and purpose.

Early in his career, Elvin Bethea had played through losing season after losing season. He even suffered through back to back 1-13 seasons. He wasn't going to let this chance slip through his fingers.

Andy Dorris wanted to remind Claudie Minor that the Astrodome turf was his territory, not Minor's.

Curley Culp wanted to punish the Broncos for trading him.

The defensive line lined up at their own 26, backs to the wall, and ready to shut this Bronco offense down.

Bethea and Dorris lambasted Otis Armstrong on first down for no gain. Take that, Claudie Minor. Take that, 1-13.

Kicker Jim Turner practiced kicks on the sideline. Curley Culp probably didn't notice. Houston had the lead. Culp wasn't going to concede a game-tying field goal without having his say.

Morton threw a flat pass to Preston which picked up 10 yards and a first down at the Houston 16. About thirteen minutes remained in the game.

Robert Brazile knew his parents were in the stands. He wasn't there to give up fourth-quarter points in front of his parents. Brazile, Bingham, and Ted Washington crashed into Denver's backfield and knocked Jim Jensen back for a 3-yard loss.

Curley Culp lined up and expected a pass on second down. Craig Morton faded back. Curley closed in. Morton froze. Culp smothered Morton at the 30-yard line. Take that, Denver Broncos.

Culp's pressure up the middle left Morton with no place to run. When pressure comes from the outside, the quarterback can step up in the pocket. Up the middle pressure often leaves the quarterback trapped with no place to go.

Two plays, and the Oiler defense bulldozed Denver back about 15 yards.

The Broncos faced a third-and-22 from the 28-yard line. Morton dropped back to pass and the venomous Oiler line surged. Three Oilers crashed down on Morton. A deafening cheer echoed through the Astrodome.

Kicker Jim Turner suffered an injury in a previous game and didn't have his normal range. The week before the wildcard, Denver signed left-footed kicker Fred Steinfort as his back up for long-range situations. Steinfort lined up for a 50-yard, game-tying field goal attempt.

The snap was good. The kick sailed deep and had the distance. The ball drifted slowly to the right. It drifted further. Bam! It bounced off the right upright. No good. Houston still had the lead.

The remarkable defensive stand included all eleven players on the field: The gang tackle on first down; Culp's sack on second; The group sack on third. Let us not forget the secondary's excellent coverage that stopped Morton from finding an open receiver under pressure. Houston's defense spun Denver's interception into Oiler momentum with an incredible stop.

"Houston Oilers Number One" blared through the Astrodome's sound system. The crowd rocked.

Gifford Nielsen and company took the field with eleven minutes left in regulation. Rob Carpenter dashed for a first down. The clock drifted under ten minutes. Tim Wilson rushed past midfield. The clock slipped under nine minutes. The Broncos forced a punt and got the ball back at their own 14 with just over eight minutes left.

The defensive stop coupled with a pair of Houston first downs equaled a big change in field position. The Oiler offense also erased three minutes from the clock. Denver still had plenty of time to tie or win, but earlier Houston's defense had shut Denver down on the Oiler 16. Now the ball sat on the complete opposite end of the field.

Larry Canada ran 13 yards for a Denver first down. The clock dipped under the eight-minute mark.

Morton faded back to pass on first down. Haven Moses cut toward the middle and was open. Morton gunned the ball his way.

Gregg Bingham snuck into the passing lane before Morton threw the ball. Bingham leapt in the air, snagged the pass, and darted toward the end zone. Offensive lineman Glenn Hyde tackled him inside the 20. Hyde's tackle likely saved a touchdown.

Just like against Miami, Bingham baited a quarterback and made an excellent catch for a late interception. Remarkably, the play produced this game's first turnover by either team.

Carpenter picked up another first down. He now averaged almost five yards per carry in Campbell's absence. The clock dropped under seven minutes. The Oilers stood at the Denver 10.

Houston ran three plays to the left behind Leon Gray. They gained about 7 yards. The plays ate up two minutes of game time. Toni Fritsch lined up for a field goal with under five minutes remaining.

Gifford Nielsen collected a high snap and placed it down with perfection. The sure-footed Toni Fritsch booted a 20-yard field goal. The Oilers led, 13-7.

A touchdown in that situation would have probably iced the game. The shoestring tackle of Gregg Bingham by Glenn Hyde was the small thread that kept Denver in the ball game. The Broncos could still win with a touchdown and extra point, and they still had plenty of time to score.

The Broncos ran a busted play on first down from their own 33 and Morton simply fell on the ball. The clock clicked under four minutes.

On second down, Otis Armstrong swept around left end. He broke a tackle and dashed down the sidelines. Only safety Mike Reinfeldt could stop him from scoring a go-ahead touchdown.

Reinfeldt kept a strong tackling angle. He frantically dove toward Armstrong. Armstrong swerved to evade Reinfeldt, but the game of inches favored Houston. Reinfeldt bumped Armstrong just enough to knock him out of bounds near midfield.

Morton looked again to hit Haven Moses on a slant pattern. This time, he ran Moses on the opposite side to avoid Gregg Bingham. The completion gained a chunk of yardage to the Houston 28.

The lead seemed in peril as Denver quickly moved the ball downfield.

Again, momentum is huge in football. Denver seemed to gain it. Momentum is a funny thing, however, and it can swing and dance a number of steps. Momentum slowed a bit as Denver fumbled the snap.

The Broncos recovered, but the fumble represented a fly in their offensive ointment as the two-minute warning appeared on the clock.

Denver committed a holding penalty coming out of the two-minute warning's gate. That created a third-and-17 from the Houston 35.

The playoffs provide an opportunity for exceptional players to make plays in crucial moments. Elvin Bethea and Curley Culp lined up for the snap. Bethea crouched down, ready to charge. He suffered through several losing seasons longing for opportunities like this.

Morton backpedaled and looked to throw. He stepped up in the pocket. Bethea used his powerful arms and shoved away his man.

Culp's man grabbed a handful of Culp's jersey, but not even a hold could stop Curley on this play.

Culp broke free and smashed into Morton's right side just as Bethea pounded a crushing blow to Morton's left side. Morton slowly got to his feet as Culp, Bethea, and the jubilant Luv Ya Blue crowd celebrated the sack.

The Broncos were down to a fourth-and-22. Houston's defense needed one more stop.

Morton took the snap. He had plenty of time to throw. Receiver Steve Watson broke down the sideline. He got open in the end zone. Morton launched a perfect pass, right on target.

Vernon Perry dashed toward Watson. He elevated himself and stretched his arms toward the ball. He caught up to it at the last possible moment and swatted it out of bounds and incomplete.

The Astrodome's decibel level approached the roar of an Apollo rocket. Perry interlocked arms with J.C. Wilson and jumped up and down in the end zone. Craig Morton sifted toward the sidelines. He placed both hands on his helmet and shook his head in disbelief.

As the clock counted down the final seconds of the Broncos' season, fans held Luv Ya Blue cards high and unleashed shouts of victory.

Lofted deep in the Astrodome's rafters still hung that simple sign that said, "We Believe."

CHAPTER 22

Divisional Round – AT SAN DIEGO

San Diego Chargers head coach Don Coryell designed an offense that heavily relied on passing. The formula blistered NFL defenses and made stars of quarterback Dan Fouts and receivers Charlie Joiner and John Jefferson. Both Joiner and Jefferson notched 1,000 yards receiving in 1979.

Rookie tight end Kellen Winslow didn't make a Hall of Fame impact yet, but tight end Bob Klein and running backs Clarence Williams and Mike Thomas also racked up considerable receiving yards.

Coryell's scheme was nicknamed, "Air Coryell" and San Diego's offense launched an air corps against opposing defenses. Quarterback Dan Fouts commandeered Coryell's aerial forces. Fouts possessed a strong arm and understood the game at a high level.

Fouts grew up in a pro football environment. His dad, Bob Fouts, announced San Francisco 49er games starting when the franchise formed in the 1940s as part of the All-American Football

Conference, better known as the AAFC. He remained the team's announcer when the 49ers joined the NFL in 1950 and stayed in that position deep into the 1960s. Young Dan Fouts worked as a 49ers ball boy and helped his dad keep stats.

San Diego drafted Fouts in the third round of the 1973 NFL Draft. His career blossomed in 1976, the sole year Bill Walsh worked as the Chargers' offensive coordinator. Things really took off for Fouts and the Chargers once Don Coryell became head coach in the middle of the 1978 season.

The team posted very high point totals for the era. San Diego often scored over 30 points per game and occasionally jetted over 40. Only the Denver Broncos prevented the Chargers from scoring under 20 points during the entire 1979 regular season.

Fouts became an NFL superstar under Don Coryell. In 1979, he surpassed Joe Namath's single-season passing yardage record. He also tied Namath for the most 300-yard passing games in a season. Fouts also set the record for most consecutive 300-yard games. He continued to set records throughout his NFL career.

Fouts threw 24 touchdown passes in 1979. He also threw 24 interceptions. Additionally, Fouts couldn't run very well and stayed in the pocket. Although Fouts proved himself a Hall of Fame quarterback, the Oilers matched up well against him. Houston's secondary led the NFL in interceptions and posted the league's third-highest sack total. Rookie Jesse Baker led the AFC in sacks with 15 ½.

Houston's offense looked very different coming into the divisional playoffs than it did approaching wildcard weekend. Injuries sidelined Earl Campbell, Dan Pastorini, and Kenny Burrough. Few onlookers gave the Oilers a chance against San Diego without those big three in the lineup.

Rob Carpenter played well in the second half against Denver and shined when called upon in the regular season. The Oilers prepared him to be the featured back against San Diego.

Until that Thursday. Carpenter sprained an ankle in practice. He now needed crutches to stand upright.

The Oilers landed in San Diego on Friday. The two teams played on Saturday.

A lot of writers glossed over the Oilers and slotted San Diego as a sure fit in the 1979 AFC Championship Game. When the two teams met in 1978, San Diego lit up the scoreboard with 45 points and over 500 yards offense. Experts, fans, and everybody's grandmother assumed San Diego would rip the Oilers like a bolt of lightning.

Game day arrived with sunny, pleasant Southern California weather.

San Diego fans also went crazy over their team. Many waved "Charger Power" signs, similar to Houston's Luv Ya Blue signs. San Diego also had their famous San Diego Chicken mascot, perhaps the most famous mascot in sports at the time.

Bum Phillips pulled his team together in the locker room. He told the team they might be low on manpower but long on guts. Rob Carpenter brought those words to life. He tossed his crutches aside, buckled his chinstrap, and stepped out on the field to play.

The Oilers won the coin toss and elected to receive.

Gifford Nielsen started at quarterback. He called Carpenter's number on third-and-short. San Diego's defense hit Carpenter a yard shy of the first down marker. He fought on with a long on guts effort and made the first down.

Mike Barber duplicated the extra effort on Houston's next third-down play. Nielsen flung a pass over the middle to Barber at midfield. The tipped ball lifted into the air and linebacker Ray Preston pelted Barber. Barber caught the ball despite the hit. He reached for a first down in San Diego territory.

The Oilers three biggest offensive stars stood on the sidelines, but the word "quit" wasn't in the Oiler playbook. Houston's offense didn't fly out to California to mope and lose. The offensive unit showed up to win. Pastorini, Campbell, and Burrough showed up to give as much vocal support as possible.

The Oilers' opening drive ended in a punt but sent an early warning to the Chargers. A trip to the 1979 AFC Championship Game wouldn't be a walk on the beach. The Oiler family rallied around adversity. The playoffs not only upped the stakes, the games upped the desire to rise to the occasion.

The Chargers started on their own 18. Houston's defense took the field with a little something extra. Not only something extra in desire, but in knowledge of San Diego's offense. Oiler defensive coordinator Ed Biles and company noticed a tell Dan Fouts gave the defense on every play.

"In studying film, we noticed Dan Fouts gave us a tell. When he had both feet together, parallel, they were going to run the ball. When he had one foot staggered behind the other, he was going to pass the ball."

Biles added that the Oiler defense had code words to communicate Charger plays to each other. "We simply called 'Army' when it was a running play and 'Air Force' when it was a passing play. We were 100% correct."

Charger Power still electrified the crowd early. Fouts surprised everyone and rifled a 34-yard pass to reserve tight end Greg McCrary on a third-and-2. McCrary only caught 5 passes during the regular season.

Fouts picked up another first down on a third-and-15 pass to a much more utilized target, John Jefferson. Fouts threw for nearly 70 yards on an opening drive that ended with a 1-yard touchdown run by Clarence Williams.

The Chargers got the ball back quickly and continued to roll. They got to midfield and faced a third-and-3. Fouts turned to Jefferson and fired the ball his way.

Vernon Perry read the route and placed himself in excellent position. He intercepted the ball. The Charger Power lights flickered as the Oiler defense generated a turnover.

The first quarter expired. The Chargers led, 7-0. The Oilers withstood the first quarter and stayed within striking distance.

San Diego, however, kept getting the ball back rather quickly. Their defensive line, led by Hall of Famer Fred Dean and Pro Bowl selection Gary "Big Hands" Johnson, kept stifling the Oilers on third down.

The Chargers started their next drive at their own 30. After two completions, they already stood at the Oiler 41.

San Diego's offense heavily used screens to running backs to spread the defense. A 10-yard screen to Clarence Williams gave San Diego their 9th first down of the game at the Oiler 31.

Points, however, owned much greater importance than first downs. "Bend, don't break" stood as an Oiler defensive cornerstone.

San Diego neared the goal line. Running back Lydell Mitchell rushed to the Oiler 6. Fouts ran Mitchell a second time and Andy Dorris dropped him for a 2-yard loss. J.C. Wilson knocked down a pass to Jefferson in the end zone on third down. The Oilers bent deeply but forced a field goal attempt.

Vernon Perry lined up inside of the right offensive tackle. Guido Merkens lined up to Perry's left, overcrowding that side. Vernon predicted Merkens might block the field goal because Merkens was lined up outside of the tackle.

San Diego snapped the ball. To Vernon's surprise, the offensive tackle instead went after Merkens.

Vernon broke into the backfield untouched and blocked the kick. The ball bounced right into his arms as an extra twist of good fortune. Perry raced down the sidelines. Defensive back Mike Fuller chased him down at the Charger 30.

Toni Fritsch followed up with a 26-yard field goal and made the score 7-3.

San Diego led, but this wasn't the pushover people expected. The Chargers collected a lot of yardage and a high number of first downs. The scoreboard, however, only reflected point totals. Perry's big play pulled the Oilers to within 4 rather than falling back by 10.

Art Stringer stopped a first-down play to help set up a third-and-9. Three minutes remained in the first half.

Elvin Bethea, Curley Culp, and Andy Dorris all closed in on Dan Fouts. Fouts rushed a throw deep down the middle to Charlie Joiner. Vernon Perry stepped in front of the pass to make his second interception of the day. He swiftly lateraled to Mike Reinfeldt, who returned it inside the Charger 40.

The defensive line had worked in conjunction with the secondary to force another Charger turnover. Opportunity knocked on the Oilers' doorstep. A score right before halftime always means a lot, especially in the playoffs. Houston even owned a chance to take a lead into the locker room, as visitors in a game nobody expected them to win.

Houston hit third down at the two-minute warning. The offense experienced trouble moving the ball against an unheralded San Diego defense that allowed the fewest points in the AFC.

A valiant play kept the drive alive.

Nielsen tossed to Carpenter just short of the first down marker on third-and-5. Carpenter bobbled the ball, but hauled it in. Defensive back Willie Buchanan hit him immediately, but Carpenter pressed on.

Linebacker Bob Horn took a shot and Carpenter spun to stay moving. Carpenter then sustained hits by defensive back Pete Shaw, and linebackers Woodrow Lowe and Ray Preston.

Literally half the defense fought Carpenter to the ground. Carpenter fought for every inch. After the play, he struggled to his feet, crawling to gather any available strength.

The officials called for a measurement. They pulled out the chain and fully extended it. The ball registered a first down. The true measurement read, "long on guts."

The players fed off each other. Carpenter's play inspired an entire team. Tim Wilson broke two tackles on the next play to secure another first down at San Diego's 17.

Gifford Nielsen looked to throw on first down. Future Hall of Famer Fred Dean flushed him out of the pocket. Dean gave chase as Nielsen escaped toward the sideline. Nielsen dashed past the 15, and past the 10. He neared the 5-yard line with a chance to step out of bounds.

Nielsen decided to go for the score. Defensive backs Mike Williams and Bo Matthews leveed hits on Nielsen and brought him down hard at the 4-yard line.

Gifford got up very slowly. The courageous play almost cost Houston their second-string quarterback. Flanker Guido Merkens, inexperienced at quarterback, was next on the depth chart.

Pastorini came onto the field and reminded Nielsen that discretion was often the better part of valor. Carl Mauck told Nielsen that he needed to stop imitating Fran Tarkenton and to get out of bounds next time. Mauck told this author that he probably used more colorful language to get his point across.

Nielsen realized he took a big risk, but the whole Houston team played inspired football. Nielsen didn't want to quit after simply getting a first down. He wanted a touchdown.

Barley over a minute remained in the first half. The Oilers had a first-and-goal on the 4. Three plays netted 3 yards.

Houston had fourth down at the 1. San Diego fans roared. Houston lined up for a field goal to trim San Diego's lead with mere seconds left in the first half.

Football takes strange turns at times. Over the course of a season, a lot of breaks even out. A few breaks repeat themselves in storybooks of magical seasons.

A magic wand certainly waved over the 1979 Houston Oilers. More magic breathed upon Houston's season on Toni Fritsch's field goal attempt.

Fritsch easily made the field goal to trim the lead to 7-6. A yellow penalty flag lay on the field, however. The Chargers placed 12 men on the field during the field goal attempt, repeating the mistake the Cowboys made on Thanksgiving Day.

In this case, however, the penalty didn't give the Oilers a first down. Accepting the penalty simply moved the ball half the distance to the goal line.

If Houston accepted the penalty, it would be fourth down on the half-yard line. The Oilers would take 3 valuable points off the scoreboard and risk handing all game momentum to San Diego going into half time. Declining the penalty made sure Houston scored on an important drive and carried something into the locker room.

Bum Phillips took a long on guts stance. He decided to go for it. A handoff to Earl Campbell almost guaranteed a touchdown, but he wasn't available. That half yard wasn't as simple now. A lot rode on that half yard, and a lot rode on getting points in that situation.

The Oilers still had All-Pro Leon Gray at left tackle. Houston sent Tim Wilson in motion toward the left side. Rob Carpenter originally lined up on the right side, but he also ran in motion to the left. That left running back Boobie Clark alone in the backfield.

Gifford Nielsen took the snap from Carl Mauck. Mauck pulled to his left as Nielsen handed Clark the ball. Clark broke to the left side. Defensive back Hal Stringert crashed into the backfield on the far-left side, but Carpenter blocked him.

Clark quickly cut inside. Linebacker Ray Preston braced himself in Clark's path at the goal line, with a clean chance to stop the play.

Carl Mauck rolled through Preston before Preston got his opportunity. Clark ducked his head and crossed over the goal line for a touchdown.

Bum Phillips threw his arms up in the air and applauded. The play worked perfectly.

Houston's coaching staff knew from game film that San Diego tended to clog the middle with big players. Phillips thought that running to the side would limit the defensive line's ability to move across the line of scrimmage, especially with Leon Gray on that side of the line. David Carter also took out a man from his left guard position.

Houston took a 10-7 lead into halftime, the exact same halftime score as the wildcard game.

A stunned San Diego crowd expressed concern after Charger Power didn't light up the first half scoreboard as expected. The home team had thirty minutes left to save a record-breaking 12-4 season.

Oiler linebacker Ted Washington almost completely dashed the home team's hopes on the first play of the second half. Washington nearly intercepted Fouts with a clear sideline in front of him. Washington might have scored.

Fouts made the Oiler defense pay for the missed opportunity. He hit Charlie Joiner for a long gain to the Oiler 45. He then hit tight end Bob Klein for another 16 yards. The officials tacked on another 15 yards against the Oilers for hitting Dan Fouts after the throw.

Lydell Mitchell scored on a rare Charger running play and San Diego regained the lead on their first possession of the second half.

Ken Burrough couldn't stand watching the game from the sidelines. He begged coaches to put him in the game as a decoy. His college track days taught him how to run without aggravating an injury. He told coaches he could coax defenders away from the ball and other receivers.

Sure enough, he drew a defender on his first play back. Tim Wilson burst up the middle for several yards. Wilson got to midfield on another carry, as Burrough took a defensive back deep downfield.

San Diego's Gary Johnson sacked Gifford Nielsen on the next play, but the cornerback covering Burrough was called for defensive holding.

So far, Burrough's decoy strategy helped move the Oilers into Charger territory. San Diego assumed Burrough entered the game as a deep play threat and had no idea his only role was to con the defense.

The drive stalled, but Houston downed the punt at the San Diego 2.

Games can change quickly after dramatic shifts in field position. San Diego owned very little margin for error with their offense cornered deep in their own territory in the third quarter of a close playoff game.

San Diego ran a few running plays and got some breathing room. Fouts returned to throwing the ball. Houston's defense returned to hitting him.

Fouts hurried a throw with Robert Brazile breathing down his neck. Brazile pounded him as he threw. On the next play, Bethea closed in with pressure from the outside and forced an incomplete pass.

The Air Coryell offense relied on a lot of precise timing between the quarterback and receivers. Curley Culp spoke about how a pass rush can ruin such precision.

"Anytime you get any kind of deep penetration in the backfield, especially if you have a quarterback standing maybe five yards deep in the pocket, that kind of disrupts his timing and creates a problem for him. As defensive linemen, we all strive to shorten the pocket for the quarterback and break his timing so he has difficulty doing the things he needs to do."

The pressure forced San Diego's first punt of the game. Rich Ellender returned the punt to the San Diego 22. Houston won a significant battle in terms of field position. The Oilers needed to spin that opportunity into points.

Gifford Nielsen spotted an open receiver in the end zone. Defensive back Mike Williams dove fully extended to make a spectacular interception. Williams looked a bit like Charger receiver John Jefferson on the play, a man known for his acrobatic catches.

San Diego adjusted to Houston's pass rush with a quick 15-yard pass on first down. Fouts used a shorter five-step drop rather than his longer seven-step.

Fouts soon ate turf again, however. Andy Dorris leveled him. Fouts staggered and got up slowly.

Elvin Bethea crashed in on the next play and popped Fouts after he threw. A holding penalty against the lineman trying to slow Bethea negated a completion.

Fouts stumbled over his own feet on the next play, a third-and-17. He hurried a throw downfield. J.C. Wilson snagged a remarkable one-handed interception. Wilson returned the ball to San Diego's 45.

Houston's pass rush dumped sugar into Air Coryell's gas tank. The secondary and linebackers provided excellent coverage downfield. Sacks, interceptions, and hurried incompletions followed.

Concerned looks appeared on the faces of San Diego's players and coaches.

Houston's offense still needed to convert their great second half field position into points, and the Oilers' three main weapons weren't fully functional. Two stood on the sidelines and the other served as a decoy.

Houston's first two plays after the interception gained nothing.

Bum Phillips made an earlier comment that coaching meant playing the hand that you're dealt. Houston didn't hold many face cards in today's hand. The team, however, didn't quit. This team was long on guts.

Houston's offensive line provided excellent protection thus far. Carpenter, Wilson, and Clark courageously filled in for Campbell. Gifford Nielsen proved he had the talent to make plays in his start against Kansas City and after he filled in for Pastorini against Cincinnati. The Oilers needed something to happen in the passing game.

Nielsen dropped into the pocket on third down. Mike Renfro was open over the middle, although he was short of the first down marker.

Nielsen threw to Renfro. Renfro shook off a tackle and sped into the open field past the first down marker. He made it past San Diego's 35-yard line and cut to the outside.

The cut forced defensive back Willie Buchanan and linebacker Ray Preston to get in each other's way. Preston slipped but continued the chase. Buchanan got caught in traffic as offensive lineman David Carter hustled downfield.

Renfro crossed the 30 as Preston gained ground. Mike Barber slowed Preston down with a block. Carl Mauck then bumped Preston completely out of the play.

Renfro crossed the 20 as linebacker Woodrow Lowe and safety Glen Edwards angled for the tackle. Ronnie Coleman had a shot a blocking one defender, but not both. Renfro pointed at Edwards. Coleman ran to block him.

The chaotic play neared the goal line.

Renfro dashed toward the pylon, running out of room against the sideline. Coleman pursued Edwards but also got in the way of Woodrow Lowe trying to make the tackle.

Lowe pushed Coleman from behind, hoping to knock Coleman into Renfro to force Renfro out of bounds inside the 5. He shoved Coleman into Edwards instead. Renfro narrowly escaped into the end zone.

The wild touchdown and extra point put the Oilers ahead, 17-14. The few Oiler fans who made the trip whistled and applauded one of the most exciting plays of 1979.

Again, the playoffs give players a chance to showcase their best skills in the most important games of the year. Renfro showed his playmaking ability after the catch. The offensive line showed their grit and hustle. Gifford Nielsen showed his determination. Mike Barber, Ronnie Coleman, and the entire offense proved they had the willpower to do whatever it takes at any moment to make something happen for the team.

Long on guts.

Dan Fouts fired away to counter the Oilers' go-ahead touchdown. He quickly moved the offense to midfield.

All week, the media had reminded everyone, including the Oilers, that Dan Founts broke this record and set that record in 1979. Elvin Bethea and the rest of the defense took the reports as a challenge to stop Fouts. Bethea talked about that added dimension to the game.

"It was the challenge. That's what I always wanted. I loved the challenge, especially when you're in the playoffs. Dan Fouts was throwing at everybody and it was, 'Dan Fouts this, and he's the greatest player to throw the ball.' That was a challenge to see all of this in the paper about how great he was and how great that team was. That challenged each one of us."

Bethea played against Fouts several times over the years. He anticipated Fouts' snap count. He timed many of Fouts' snaps perfectly and gained an extra split second coming off the line.

Bethea interrupted this particular drive as he rushed through the line and piled on top of Fouts before the play developed. The quarterback slowly gathered himself as the third quarter ended.

Fifteen minutes remained in a game that few thought Houston could keep close, let alone win.

The fourth quarter started like the third quarter ended, and Dan Fouts took a hit. Jesse Baker wrapped him up as he threw the ball, forcing another incompletion.

Dan Fouts was tough. He took the punishment. The hits hurt badly, but Fouts wanted to win. He hit John Jefferson for a 19-yard gain to keep the drive alive.

The Charger Power crowd came back to life, but the Oiler defense stiffened and stopped the drive.

Rob Carpenter demonstrated guts again by plowing through the San Diego defense. He fought his way through three tackles to pick up 10 yards. The man who needed crutches to walk the night before proved that his will to win outdistanced the pain.

Clark then picked up another first down. The clock ticked under nine minutes. Carpenter fought for yet another first down, getting inside San Diego territory.

Houston's drive stalled, but the punt left San Diego at their own 10 with less than seven minutes left. Although points mattered most, the minutes shaved off the clock loomed largely in the Oilers favor.

Fouts immediately fired a pass to Charlie Joiner. That put San Diego in Houston territory.

Bingham and Dorris answered on the next play and sacked Fouts at the Charger 46. Fouts responded with a pass to the Oiler 35. The game solidified into a classic matchup of an outstanding offense against a fantastic defense.

Fouts countered with an even quicker three-step drop and immediately gunned a pass over the middle.

The ball bounced off tight end Bob Klein's hands and popped straight into the air. Robert Brazile tipped it and Vernon Perry snatched it for his third interception of the day.

Just over three minutes remained on the clock. Charger Power's grid felt a shockwave.

Nielsen drained the clock to the two-minute warning. He took the snap on the ensuing play, a third-and-7, and completed a pass to Ronnie Coleman for the first down.

San Diego reached into their timeout wallet and spent the first of their valuable timeouts. The clock billed the Chargers for their remaining timeouts before Houston punted.

Dan Fouts and crew took over at their own 5-yard line. Fouts' dangerous arm wounded defenses on a moment's notice, but San Diego lacked timeouts.

He quickly got San Diego near their own 30.

The Oilers' pass rush stepped up and forced a hurried throw on the next play. Linebacker Robert Brazile's man-to-man coverage on receiver John Jefferson also helped shut down the play. Few linebackers keep up with top receivers, but Brazile matched the task.

Jefferson got open on the next play and the Chargers got to their own 41. Brazile still made a difference and tackled Jefferson in bounds. Precious seconds slipped away.

In those days, NFL rules did not allow quarterbacks to spike the ball to stop the clock. Fouts quickly rushed an incompletion with only ten seconds left.

Ten seconds left in a game that few outside of Harris County gave the Oilers even a prayer to win. Ten seconds to Charger Power's offensive juggernaut being unplugged for the season. Ten seconds to the top seed in the AFC playoffs being upset at home.

Fouts threw deep to Joiner in a frantic final attempt to regain electricity in Chargerland. Vernon Perry shut down Air Coryell's power grid for good with yet another interception.

Robert Brazile praises Vernon's efforts. "Let's give credit where credit is due," Brazile said. "Mister Vernon Perry. When I think about the game he had, I get chill bumps. The guy blocked a field goal, picked it up and ran for 60-some yards, and he got 4 interceptions, which is still today a league record for interceptions in a playoff game.

"To be a part of that, to be a witness of that, no one can ever take that away from me. And to know Vernon like a brother and to share that with him, that makes me feel good knowing that he was my brother from Jackson State and my teammate with the Houston Oilers."

In a season that Dan Fouts set many records, it was Houston's Vernon Perry who claimed the postseason record for most interceptions in a game with 4. As Brazile pointed out, the record still stands today.

Records are made to be broken. Win-loss records, however, remain permanently etched in history. The Oilers 1-0 record against San Diego in 1979 stands forever. The victory remains one of the toughest and most cherished wins in franchise history.

Bum Phillips raised his hand in the locker room. Players gathered around to listen. He reminded his team that the manpower might be short, but the Oilers were long on guts.

Soon afterward, an unlikely visitor knocked on the Oilers' locker room door. It was Charger head coach Don Coryell.

Andy Dorris remembered the moment: "Don Coryell came into our locker room afterwards and congratulated us on showing what tough was."

The Oilers defined what tough was and what long on guts meant. Vernon Perry – long on guts. Rob Carpenter – long on guts. The entire offensive line, the defensive line, Gifford Nielsen, the linebacking corps – long on guts.

Every player that stepped on that field with an oil derrick pasted to their helmet revealed what it meant to wear a Columbia blue Houston Oiler uniform in 1979.

Bum Phillips told reporters that Houston's win over San Diego wasn't a character builder, it was a character finder. For sixty minutes, a tight-knit group of men not only defined toughness, courage, and swagger, they also painted a portrait of the fortitude and willpower that resided within each individual.

Sports gives participants a rare opportunity to learn their own character and know their true selves when everything is on the line. The NFL playoffs magnify such characteristics within each player and the team itself. The Houston Oilers proved who they were to themselves, their teammates, and the hallways of history.

The Pittsburgh Steelers toppled Miami the following day.

The AFC playoffs came down to a rematch of the 1978 AFC Championship Game between two teams that many considered the best in pro football.

Both teams knew they could win. Both teams knew they were in for a battle.

CHAPTER 23

1979 AFC Championship Game –
AT PITTSBURGH

Earl Campbell and Dan Pastorini reveled in the Oiler victory, despite not getting to play.

Campbell was tired of people saying that if you stopped Earl Campbell, then you beat the Oilers. He added that people often said the same about Pastorini. Those theories miserably failed the litmus test when the Oilers defeated San Diego with Campbell and Pastorini sidelined.

Pastorini told reporters that he couldn't have been prouder of Gifford Nielsen if Gifford were his own son.

The biggest question of the week was if Pastorini and Campbell could play against the Steelers.

Campbell's injury reportedly wasn't as severe as Pastorini's. Rumors swirled even before the San Diego game that Campbell might be ready to play.

Campbell was listed as probable against the Steelers. Pastorini was listed as questionable.

Pastorini says Bum Phillips asked him if he thought he could play. "Bum came to me and said, 'How are you?' I said about 80 percent, which I was lying because I was about 60 percent. He said, 'Well, you at 80 percent is better than what I got at 100%. I need you out there if you can play.'

"I said, 'I'll play.'"

A groin pull the extent of Pastorini's usually takes about six weeks to heal. Pastorini played the 1978 AFC Championship Game with broken ribs. He played in the rematch several weeks before his groin injury healed.

Players playing hurt in the playoffs wasn't unusual. Many players fought through some sort of injury. Several of Pastorini's teammates planned to tough things out for the AFC Championship, including Earl Campbell, Rob Carpenter, and Mike Barber.

In the opposite locker room, Lynn Swann didn't know if a hamstring injury would keep him out of action. In the NFC, the Rams' Jack Youngblood played through playoffs with a broken leg.

You might remember that Pastorini stopped talking to local sportswriter Dale Robertson mid-season. This wasn't the first time a Houston quarterback distanced himself from the media.

In the 1960s, George Blanda stopped speaking with two *Houston Post* writers after hearing their criticisms. Although Pastorini's situation with Robertson was unusual, it wasn't unprecedented.

On the week leading up to the AFC Championship, Robertson used Pastorini quotes he heard on a recording. Afterward, Pastorini told Robertson to never quote him unless the two of them spoke directly. Robertson got upset and reportedly used profanity to underscore his feelings.

Meanwhile, Bum Phillips spoke to another reporter outside. Bum told the reporter that the Oilers never had any problems with the media.

Suddenly a door flung open. Pastorini physically threw Robertson out the door. The writer landed in the middle of Phillips' interview.

Bum calmly added, "Until now" to his previous statement.

The incident created all kinds of headlines. Papers printed photographs of the episode unfolding. Overall, though, people made light of the event more than they made waves. It was a different time. There wasn't social media. There wasn't a 24-hour news cycle to analyze things. The short encounter didn't stay in the papers long, and a fair share of the reporting was lighthearted.

One Steeler joked that Pittsburgh's players would never throw a sportswriter through a door. They preferred to throw sportswriters through walls. Terry Bradshaw reportedly joked around with Robertson about the scuffle. Pastorini practiced with a jersey that said, "Rocky," the name of a popular boxing movie starring Sylvester Stallone.

The movie's sequel, *Rocky II*, came out in 1979. Like the film, the upcoming AFC Championship Game featured a rematch of a perennial champion against a tenacious underdog contender.

At the time, the Steelers were the only team to have won three Super Bowls, and they did it in a short five-year span. They also stood as the NFL's reigning champions.

The Oilers represented the courageous underdog that never quit. Houston won close games, scrapped together by grit and willpower rather than eye-popping stats. A lot of teams outgained Houston and piled on first downs but still lost by a points decision.

Pittsburgh, like Houston, held an enthusiastic fan base. Fans waved "Terrible Towels" designed by broadcaster Myron Cope. Banners draped the rails of Three Rivers Stadium. Many signs represented fan clubs for individual players such as "Franco's Italian Army" for Franco Harris and "Lambert's Lunatics" for Jack Lambert. Steeler fans screamed the "Here we go, Steelers" chant and sang Steeler-themed songs. Both cities took great pride in their football teams.

The Oilers-Steelers rivalry stood in contrast to many other rivalries. Unlike other classic rivalries of the '70s, cheap shots were rare. The Steelers-Raiders rivalry got so nasty that the teams ended up in court.

Also, the Steelers and Oilers held the other in high regard. The Steelers once sent briefcases to the Oilers as a gift after Houston knocked the Bengals out of playoff contention. Steeler fans sent Bum Phillips dozens of cowboy hats after learning his hat was stolen after a game in Pittsburgh. Players on both sides remain good friends to this day.

For three hours on game day, however, the two teams battled hard. The Steelers and Oilers brought out the best rather than the worst in each other. Each team pressed the other to play up to its highest potential. As evidenced in Week 2, the Steelers played some of their best games against Houston, and like in 1978 on *Monday Night Football*, the Oilers played some of their best games against Pittsburgh.

The Oilers' win over San Diego shocked many people but the Steeler organization likely wasn't surprised. Both teams knew the sequel to the 1978 AFC Championship Game stood a good chance to be made, complete with the original cast, a sold-out box office, and a national audience ready for a live screening.

Weather for the 1979 AFC Championship Game proved quite better than 1978's conditions, although the field crew chipped away ice on one side of the field before game time. That ice created dicey footing in one red zone.

Other than that, it was a typical cold, overcast, wintery day at Three Rivers Stadium in Pittsburgh, where the Steelers had won 15 straight games after losing to Houston on *Monday Night Football* in 1978. Pittsburgh won 23 of their last 24 in their own palace and were the only NFL team to not lose at home in 1979.

NBC's pregame host Bryant Gumbel said this game likely stood as the real Super Bowl. Many football writers agreed. After all, the Steelers were the reigning champions and the Oilers defeated both teams from Super Bowl 13 in the regular season.

Elvin Bethea stepped onto the field knowing that this might be his last chance to make the Super Bowl. The Oilers drafted him in 1968 and this was his twelfth year in the league. He made the Pro Bowl but also suffered a few injuries that hampered his playing time. He wanted to win this game badly.

Like with Dan Fouts, Bethea knew Steeler quarterback Terry Bradshaw's tendencies. He probably knew Bradshaw better, having played against him much more often. He anticipated Bradshaw's snap count well.

The Steelers got the ball first and had a third-and-3 on their opening series. Elvin dug his shoes into the turf and crouched into his three-point stance.

He jumped off the line. He had a shot at Bradshaw and swung at him. Bradshaw ducked and completed a pass to John Stallworth at Houston's 41-yard line for a first down.

Bradshaw's escape actually helped the Oilers in the end. Instead of punting, they got a new series of downs. On third-and-4, Bradshaw faded back again. Bethea bullrushed and nearly pushed tackle Ted Petersen into Bradshaw.

Bradshaw spotted tight end Bennie Cunningham downfield and fired a pass.

Vernon Perry stepped in front and made another postseason interception. He took off with the ball and had plenty of open turf in front of him. He angled toward the sideline much like he did when returning the blocked kick against San Diego. This time, however, Vernon dashed all the way to the end zone.

The Oilers led 7-0 before fans had a chance to settle into their stadium blankets. Noisy Three Rivers Stadium fell silent in disbelief.

Pittsburgh hoped to establish their running game early. Running backs Franco Harris and Rocky Bleier combined to pick up a couple of first downs on their next possession. Houston then forced a third-and-5.

Bradshaw backpedaled and looked to throw. The pocket began to collapse from the outside and Bradshaw ran up the middle. Bethea wouldn't let Bradshaw escape his grasp a second time and dragged Bradshaw down for the sack.

Two possessions for Pittsburgh yielded a Houston defensive score and a punt. Houston's defense needed this kind of game to win at Pittsburgh.

The Oilers found tough sledding offensively. Pastorini took a couple of steps back to throw, but L.C. Greenwood immediately toppled him for a sack. Houston couldn't manage a first down against the Steel Curtain. The crowd returned to life, inspired by the Steeler defense. Houston punted from their own end zone.

The punt made it to the Houston 40. Bum Phillips earlier said that field position might ultimately decide the game. So far, the Steelers owned both the home field advantage and the field position advantage. Houston's 7-0 lead looked tenuous, especially considering that gamebreaker Lynn Swann fought through his injury to play.

The Oiler pass rush continued to pressure Bradshaw. This time, however, the mobile quarterback rolled to the sideline and snuck all the way to the Houston 4. Houston needed a championship defense to keep the lead.

Several Oilers crushed Franco Harris on first down. Art Stringer tackled Sidney Thornton on second. Two plays, zero yards. On third down, Vernon Perry charged on a safety blitz. Bradshaw threw high.

The Oiler defense proved itself with a goal-line stand to force a field goal attempt.

Matt Bahr's field goal made it 7-3. Both teams gave themselves something to build on early, but the Oilers defense pocketed a touchdown and a stiff rebuke inside the 5. The Houston lead withstood an early punch from the reigning champions.

Pittsburgh leveled Earl Campbell for a 4-yard loss on first down. Houston's offense needed to make plays. Campbell struggled, and Pastorini was sacked on Houston's only pass play.

Tim Wilson provided Houston's first offensive jab. Pastorini tossed a screen to him on the left sideline. Wilson evaded three tacklers and hustled all the way into Pittsburgh territory. Carl Mauck provided a key block to extend the play. Houston unfastened at least one bolt in the Steeler defense.

The Steelers kept smothering Campbell for losses. They gang tackled him up the middle. They doubled up on him running to his left. They piled four tacklers on him as he ran to his right. Joe Greene burst through the line to stuff Campbell on second down.

That set up another third-and-long for the Oiler offense.

The offensive line gave Pastorini solid protection on third down. He spotted Ronnie Coleman downfield. Pastorini threw into double coverage, and the pass dropped right into Coleman's hands near the Pittsburgh 10.

Houston didn't need pretty drives to beat Pittsburgh. They simply needed points. In this case, a pair of completions offset the suffocating run defense.

The first quarter ended, and the Oilers had the lead. They knocked on the Steel door with an opportunity for more points.

Houston kicked a field goal and led, 10-3. The scrappy Oilers compiled a 72-yard drive despite owning a negative net rushing total for the game.

The Steelers, however, established their running game early. Bradshaw took advantage and threw on first down. He hit Lynn Swann at the 50.

Immediately, the Steelers had the ball at midfield after Houston's field goal. Swann soon caught another pass inside the Oiler 20. That set up Bradshaw hitting Cunningham in the back of the end zone for a score.

Just like that, the game was tied. Three Rivers Stadium rumbled with cheers.

Houston turned to the screen pass, but the Steelers adjusted and stopped it for a 1-yard loss.

Pastorini looked deeper on second down. He found Renfro over the middle and struck for a 12-yard gain. Joe Greene pummeled Pastorini as he threw, but the Oilers had the ball at their own 40.

At this point in the game, Pastorini was a perfect 5-for-5 passing. The Oilers were tied with Pittsburgh halfway through the second quarter and driving downfield. Had Bum Phillips known all of this before the game started, he certainly would have liked his chances.

Bum knew the Oilers had to play mistake-free football. An extremely thin margin for error existed playing against the Steelers at home in the playoffs. At this point, only the undefeated 1972 Miami Dolphins beat the Steelers in a playoff game at Pittsburgh during the 1970s.

Houston needed to establish a running game. An effective passing attack, however, could force the Steelers to spread their defense to compensate and improve the running game's chance of success.

Bum always said the Oilers weren't pretty dancers, but they danced every dance. The offense chugged along but still found ways to sustain the previous drive for a field goal. The current drive also held nice potential.

For now, the Steel Curtain continued to crush Houston's running game. They placed seven defenders on the line of scrimmage, with Jack Lambert lined up close behind. The formation combined to hamper the running game and provide a substantial pass rush.

The alignment forced a third-and-12. Pastorini hit Guido Merkens on the sidelines for a first down. Or so it seemed. A penalty erased the play.

The Oiler line again gave Pastorini time to throw on the next play. He found Mike Renfro downfield. Renfro caught the ball inside Pittsburgh territory and gained even more yards than Merkens' original play.

Renfro ran downfield, but safety Donnie Shell punched the ball loose from behind. The ball bounced directly toward defensive back Mel Blount. Blount recovered the fumble and returned it to the Houston 48.

Two Oiler mistakes and the Steelers stopped the drive. Pittsburgh enjoyed great field position. Houston's defense had their backs to the wall again.

In the 1978 AFC Championship Game, Pittsburgh scored 17 points in the last two minutes of the first half and took a commanding 31-3 lead. The Oilers didn't want to repeat the scenario of turnovers and botched plays that fueled that disaster. Houston fought so hard all season to get back to this point. They knew they were an even better team this year.

Bradshaw sensed the possibility of a Steeler scoring explosion and threw deep for Swann in the end zone. J.C. Wilson made a terrific play to bat the ball aside.

Pittsburgh returned to running Harris and Bleier and drove down the short field. Bradshaw then hit Stallworth for a 20-yard touchdown. Terrible Towels swung from the fists of Steeler fans.

Pittsburgh led, 17-10.

The two-minute warning hit, and the Steelers subsequently hit Pastorini. Donnie Shell blasted through the line on a safety blitz and swatted Pastorini's hand. The smacked throw lofted straight into the air and almost into the arms of L.C. Greenwood. The Oilers avoided disaster on the play, but it appeared eerily similar to the events of the final two minutes of 1978's first half.

The Oilers weren't as fortunate on the next play. Pastorini's pass sailed into the arms of rookie defensive back Dwayne Woodruff.

Houston's defense needed a big stop again to keep within one score at halftime.

With twenty-one seconds left, Pittsburgh picked up the exact 9 yards needed for a first down, and Franco Harris stepped out of bounds to stop the clock. Such clock management set the Steelers apart from other teams in the 1970s.

The ball lay just outside Matt Bahr's field goal range. Bradshaw next turned to Rocky Bleier who got the ball inside the 20 and dashed out of bounds to stop the clock with seven seconds left in the first half.

The Steelers were in perfect position to score, but Matt Bahr's field goal attempt veered wide left.

The Oilers did what they needed to do and kept the game within one score. The team didn't succumb to a flurry of turnovers in the closing minutes of the first half as they did in 1978. Houston hammered a wooden stake in the ground that held on by a missed field goal.

The Oilers needed only one big play or a clutch drive to tie the game. If the Oilers avoided mistakes and got a key play, the possibilities were endless.

The Oilers proved time and time again that games could turn their way if they just hung around long enough for a turnover like John Riggins' fumble in Week 1, a wild play like Mike Renfro's touchdown against San Diego, or a crucial mistake like the 12-men on the field penalty against the Cowboys.

With Earl Campbell. a big play could happen at any moment. Just ask the Dallas Cowboys, Miami Dolphins, or Baltimore Colts.

The Oilers' pass rush could build a surge and stop an offensive rally cold. Just ask the Denver Broncos.

And the secondary? Well, Vernon Perry already scored a touchdown in the game.

Dan Pastorini's arm toasted the Raiders secondary and ruined the Cowboys' Thanksgiving plans.

Toni Fritsch's foot kicked the decisive points in 5 regular season games and 1 playoff. The Oilers won all 6 of those games by 3 points or fewer.

Bum Phillips built a scrappy team that thrived on adversity, fought for each other like family, and above all refused to quit. Those qualities won a lot of games on scoreboards even though the Oilers looked subpar on the stat sheet. If the ball bounced Houston's way a time or two, then the same thing could happen in Pittsburgh if the Oilers found a way to stay in the neighborhood long enough.

The Steelers bested the Oilers in total rushing yards and yards per attempt during the regular season, finishing second in the NFL in rushing yards and first in yards per carry.

The same held true in the first half of the AFC Championship Game. The Steelers rushed for 101 net yards in the first half compared to the Oilers' 2. That's right, 2 yards rushing in the first half.

The Steelers mainly featured future Hall of Fame running back Franco Harris and tough Vietnam veteran Rocky Bleier in their backfield. Their trap plays fit right in Harris' running style.

"They were primarily a trapping team. They trapped all the time," Andy Dorris said. "One of the coaches said, 'They trap so much, they're trapping when they get of the plane!' He was making a joke as to how good they were at it. They played really low to the ground, and the back was hitting the hole at the same time you were engaging the guard."

Oiler linebacker Gregg Bingham added, "And if you run a 1-35 bluff trap and the defensive line is slanting towards it, (the runner) has to carry it another hole further out. If the defensive line was slanted the other way, you have to carry it another hole in.

"That's what Franco Harris was so good at. He would actually sort of tippy-toe and wait for the hole to open. He was very patient. Franco Harris is one of the best trapping backs to ever play the game because he understood how it worked. He was patient when he needed to be patient, and he hit the hole like a bullet when he needed to. He knew there was a difference in the gears."

Overall, the Steelers outgained the Oilers nearly two-to-one in the first half, but Houston kept close on the scoreboard.

The Oilers received the opening kickoff of the second half and hoped to make something happen in the first five minutes to swing momentum their way. Handoffs to Wilson and Campbell quickly earned a first down. So far, so good.

Joe Greene dampened the Oiler ground game on the next play, however. Greene looked like he lined up in the backfield and knocked Campbell for a 2-yard loss.

Cliff Parsley punted the ball back to Pittsburgh. The Steelers would likely open the second half with good field position. It seemed like a disappointing start to Houston's second half.

The Steelers misjudged the punt, however, and fumbled. David Carter recovered for the Oilers at the Steeler 41. Houston scored a huge break.

Pastorini called a play-action pass. He rifled the ball over the middle to Mike Barber. Defensive end Steve Furness toppled Pastorini as he launched the ball.

The ball flew high, but Barber leapt and got his hands on it at the 16-yard line. A punishing hit from defensive back Mel Blount knocked the ball incomplete.

On the next play, Joe Greene again lined up in the backfield and smashed Campbell for a 4-yard loss.

A dropped pass on a slant route spoiled a potential big gain on third down. The receiver likely heard Jack Lambert's footsteps. Three plays, three Hall of Fame defensive players, and Houston's golden opportunity turned to rust against the Steel Curtain.

The Oilers gained significant field position, however. Parsley's punt shoved Pittsburgh back to their own 13.

Houston matched Pittsburgh's defensive efforts by subverting Steeler run attempts on first and second down. On third-and-7, Andy Dorris sacked Terry Bradshaw at the Steeler 9.

The Steelers punted from their own end zone, and the Oilers started with great field position for the second time in a row. The Oilers received a second chance in another key moment of the 1979 season. Houston's offense stood only 51 yards away from a game-tying touchdown.

Earl Campbell ran left. For a moment, it looked like he could turn the corner and get at least 10-15 yards. Cornerback Ron Johnson somehow caught up to Campbell and pushed him out of bounds.

The officials flagged Johnson for a 5-yard incidental facemask penalty. The Oilers had a first-down-and-5 inside Pittsburgh territory.

Pastorini tossed to Barber again on second down. He had great protection and made a fine throw. Barber again got his hands on the ball but the punishing Steeler secondary laid another direct hit on him and forced the incompletion.

A screen to Rob Carpenter set up a fourth-and-2 on the Steeler 36. Bum turned to Earl. Campbell ran left and picked up the first down.

A late flag pushed the ball back 5 yards, however, and the Oilers' first down downgraded into a fourth-and-7. The play marked the second time the Oilers lost a first down to penalty and the second time in a row that good field position yielded nothing on the scoreboard.

The Steeler rush forced a short punt. Pittsburgh started at their 20.

Houston lost its grip on field position but the Oiler defense didn't lose its grip on the Steeler offense. Houston held Pittsburgh to 1 yard and forced yet another punt with a three-and-out.

Steeler punter Craig Colquitt lined a 66-yard punt all the way to the Houston 13.

A simple penalty on Houston's previous drive erased an Oiler first down on the Steeler 35. The penalty, combined with the massive punt, helped place Pittsburgh in the field position captain's chair.

Houston trailed by 7 and couldn't gain traction even when they started drives at midfield. How could they get anything started inside their own 20?

Earl Campbell caught a screen pass for 10 yards and a first down. Steve Furness leveled Pastorini a second time. Pastorini reeled in pain and struggled to his feet. Trainers helped him off the field.

Gifford Nielsen stepped into the Oiler huddle. He tossed a screen to Tim Wilson, who picked up 9 yards. Pastorini ran back onto the field after missing one play.

Success on the screens opened the running game a bit. Earl Campbell ran off tackle for several yards, but he fumbled on the play.

The ball bounced through the hands of a pair of Steelers and squirted downfield. Mike Renfro dove on it and recovered at the Houston 48. In the NFL, you take yards any way you can, especially on the road.

Pastorini calmly faded back and found Renfro open over the middle at the Steeler 23. Renfro held on to the catch despite a brutal blow by Jack Lambert.

Houston positioned itself to narrow the lead with a field goal or even tie the game with a touchdown. A game-tying drive after being down on the canvas at their own 13 would have made a huge statement on the road in Pittsburgh and could have given the Oilers tremendous momentum going into the fourth quarter.

Just over two minutes remained in the third quarter. Houston dominated the quarter in terms of possession. The Steelers ran six plays total and didn't make a single first down. The Steelers' biggest play of the quarter was a 66-yard punt, now on the verge of being equalized by the lengthy Oiler drive.

Houston faced a third-and-7 on the Pittsburgh 20. At this point, the Oilers stood 1-for-7 on third downs.

Pastorini quickly dropped back. Steeler Dennis Winston decked Pastroini as he lofted a pass to Ronnie Coleman on the sideline. Coleman jumped and made a tremendous catch over linebacker Loren Toews for a first-and-goal on the Steeler 7-yard line.

As the play unfolded, Lambert stumbled over Pastorini, and planted a knee in Pastorini's helmet. Lambert's move wasn't flagrant; Lambert had his back to Pastorini watching Coleman's catch.

The combination of the vicious hit by Wintson and the added blow to the head took a lot out of Pastorini, who already missed one play on the drive after being pummeled by Furness. Pastorini knelt on all fours on the cold Pittsburgh turf. Mike Barber helped him to his feet. Pastorini limped into the huddle, trying to walk off the pain.

The game and the drive fit perfectly within the Oilers' 1979 persona. Show up. Play hard. Hold on until something happens. Being down doesn't mean being out. It doesn't matter how you get the yards, just get 'em. Above all, don't quit. When your backs are against the wall, don't quit. When you haven't moved the ball all half and your next drive starts at your own 13, pick up and move on.

Those values brought the Oilers to this moment. They didn't quit in Cincinnati after being down 24 points. They didn't quit at Dallas and at Washington after being down 11. They didn't quit at San Diego when most teams would have folded without their star players.

Now, they stood with a first-and-goal at Pittsburgh in the waning moments of the third quarter in the AFC Championship Game. Seven yards between the line of scrimmage and a tie game going into the fourth quarter. Anything could happen.

The 1979 Houston Oilers lived in a world of unpredictability. The season flourished on uncanny opportunities and weird circumstances. Toni Fritsch's game-winning field goal attempt bouncing off the upright and in against Cincinnati. The strange coincidence of two 12-men on the field penalties that led to critical Houston touchdowns. A coin toss flipped Houston's way to start overtime against the Jets that sparked a game-winning drive.

Strange twists, turns, and odd bounces of an oval-shaped ball add elements of chance to a game that ideally gets decided by muscle, blood, sweat, strategy, and guts. When the chips of fate fall as they may, sometimes they fall your way. Sometimes they fall into your opponent's lap. Sometimes they fall off the table.

Dan Pastorini scraped himself together after the brutal hits. He gritted his teeth and gathered his strength as he walked to the line of scrimmage. He surveyed the defense.

He noted one-on-one coverage against Mike Renfro to his right, against defensive back Ron Johnson. He called an audible, a pass to Renfro up top. He took the snap from Carl Mauck and threw a lightning quick pass to Renfro in the end zone.

The rest, as they say, is history.

CHAPTER 24

The Renfro Play

The 1977 season landed NFL officials in some hot water. A handful of missed calls affected the outcomes of important games. Whisperings of legalizing instant replay to confirm or overturn calls gained volume. Three plays in 1977 illustrated the effect replay (or lack thereof) could have on the entire season.

In October of 1977, the Oilers recovered an apparent fumble in the end zone for a game-winning touchdown against the Bengals. The officials ruled otherwise. NFL Commissioner Pete Rozelle formally apologized for the officiating mistake made evident by video replay. The Oilers narrowly missed the playoffs, and the ruling possibly cost Houston a tie for the 1977 AFC Central Division championship.

During 1977's final week, Baltimore quarterback Bert Jones lost an apparent fumble on a busted play against New England. The officials ruled no fumble and the Colts soon scored a game-winning touchdown that lifted them into the playoffs over the Miami Dolphins.

A play in the 1977 AFC Championship Game headlined the trio of calls. NBC's video replay clearly showed Denver running back Rob Lytle fumbled near the Raider goal line. Oakland defensive lineman Mike McCoy recovered, but officials ruled Lytle was down before Raider defenders jarred the ball loose. The Broncos scored a touchdown on the next play, giving them a 14-3 lead in a game that they eventually won by 3 points.

When reporters asked Raider coach John Madden about the controversial call, he famously responded, "What controversy? It was a fumble. There's no controversy about it."

Denver had their own beef with the officials, as a potential Jack Dolbin touchdown reception would have made the score 21-3. Video replay suggested that Dolbin likely caught the ball, but it was ruled incomplete.

That call didn't gain as much attention as the no-fumble call, as many thought the latter cost the Raiders a second-straight trip to the Super Bowl.

The NFL responded with two decisions.

First, the league experimented with instant replay during the 1978 preseason, in a limited amount of nationally televised games. The replays didn't change any calls on the field, but NFL head official Art McNally supervised potentially reversible calls.

Secondly, the NFL placed an additional official on the field during games. The new official, called the side judge, stayed as a permanent addition to officiating crews.

Owners voted down permanent installation of instant replay. The league decided that the number of cameras needed to verify calls proved too costly.

Commissioner Pete Rozelle stated that the NFL didn't want to be at the television camera's mercy, and that video replay would greatly extend the length of games and possibly raise more questions than answers. He rhetorically asked about situations where an official might notice a penalty while reviewing a fumble.

Rozelle's comments failed to quiet the replay debate. The media wrote stories about replay's potential. Fans pointed at television screens. Viewers not only played armchair quarterback, but also armchair referee.

The NFL's point about the unfeasible cost of installing enough cameras to make replay effective was likely a fair assessment at the time. Television networks employed few cameras compared with today's coverage. Viewers exclusively saw camera angles from one side of the field – the same side as the press box. By the late 1970s, networks also had cameras behind the end zone. That was pretty much it.

You didn't get reverse angles, zoomed shots from the pylon, or overhead cameras. The NFL decided that instant replay required at least 12 cameras on the field, far more than networks implemented at the time.

When the Oilers lined up for a first-and-goal at the Steeler 7, NBC showed the view from the left side of the Oiler formation. Pastorini took a quick step back and tossed to Mike Renfro on the right side, far away from the camera.

Renfro had a step on cornerback Ron Johnson. Renfro grabbed the ball out of the air and landed with his feet in bounds. The play clearly looked like a touchdown to millions of viewers.

Don Orr worked as the side judge and was the nearest official to the play on the right sideline. He thought he saw ball movement at some point during the catch but didn't know if Renfro collected the ball before his feet landed in bounds.

Renfro looked at Orr and waited for a call.

According to *Sports Illustrated*, Orr told Renfro that he needed help making the call.

Orr's answer upset Renfro, who angrily told Orr that he got paid to make calls and he needed to make one.

Orr called for another official who, in theory, was responsible for watching foot placement while Orr watched for possession. The second official informed Orr that he couldn't offer any help with the call.

Mike Barber stood at the goal line after the play and shared a similar story based on what he remembered. "I heard one (official) say, 'I didn't see it.' He asked the other who said, 'Neither did I.'"

Players swarmed around the officials to make their case. Center Carl Mauck walked up to an official he knew from his college, Southern Illinois University.

Mauck said, "The guy from my school, Southern Illinois University, he was a Marine Corps officer, and he was a good guy but he was on that call. (*Laughs*) I went right up to him and he said, 'Get away from me!' I said, 'Get away, hell, you make the right call!' I went over to (Jim) Tunney because he was the referee and I said, 'Don't blow it! We scored!' I had a great view of it. He caught the ball inbounds."

Rich Caster clearly saw Renfro's reception from the opposite side of the end zone. "If you turn it around, there are a couple other angles from the other side of the field that you can see me in the back of the end zone. I ran an identical route," Caster said. "Now, they threw it to the right guy, I'm not saying they should have thrown to me. Mike Renfro was absolutely a pressure receiver.

"From what I could see, it was clear and without question a touchdown. It was a good catch. I saw it that Sunday. I was right in there arguing with them. Obviously, the officials weren't going to be interested in hearing what we had to say."

The officials huddled together to discuss what call to make. Pastorini cleared his teammates away, mindful of a possible penalty. He turned to Jim Tunney and said, "Come on, Jim, you know it's a touchdown. You gotta give it to us."

Meanwhile, NBC showed slow-motion replays that conclusively showed Renfro's feet landed in bounds. Renfro also looked to have possession of the ball gauging from the two replay angles NBC had. Announcers Dick Enberg and Merlin Olsen walked viewers through the play. Millions watched the play over and over and each time it looked more and more like a touchdown to many of those viewers.

Phil Tuckett worked the game as a cameraman for NFL Films. As noted previously, he knew Bum Phillips well. Tuckett not only knew Bum from working at NFL Films, but he also knew Bum from when he briefly played with the San Diego Chargers while Phillips worked as an assistant.

NFL Films allowed Phil Tuckett greater flexibility with his camera than broadcasting networks. NFL Films allowed Tuckett to move freely about Three Rivers Stadium to catch the best angles possible. Tuckett ignored the broadcasting networks' ideas that cameras needed to solely catch footage from the press box side of the field.

Over the course of Tuckett's career, his hunches led to amazing shots of famous plays. For example, he guessed the only chance for a possible highlight at the end of an Eagles-Giants game would be to face the defense from the end zone. The Giants fumbled away a sure win, and Tuckett captured the famous shot of Eagle defensive back Herman Edwards scoring the winning touchdown in the game known as, "The Miracle at the Meadowlands."

Tuckett was a former pro football player who understood the game. When the Oilers lined up for the first-and-goal at the 7, Tuckett acted upon one of his hunches. He remembered times when

Houston threw to the right corner of the end zone in similar situations. He dashed over to film from the right side of the end zone, rather than the press box side.

The action came right toward him.

He focused in on Renfro as the play happened right in front of his camera. Tuckett caught a crucial angle, although the film wouldn't be developed until well after the game.

Over a minute passed and the officiating crew still hadn't given a call. They discussed what to do but had only one opportunity to view the play -- live as it occurred. Rules prohibited them to use video replay at all.

Referee Jim Tunney needed to make a decision without much information. Fans knew what they saw on their televisions. The officiating crew wasn't sure what they'd seen.

Jim Tunney eventually emerged from the officials meeting. He made one simple motion and declared the pass incomplete.

The scenario ironically created the exact same confusion Commissioner Rozelle feared. The Renfro Play greatly extended the time it took for the officials to make a call. The process to make the call raised more questions than answers. The NFL indeed found itself at the mercy of the camera, in one of the three most important games of the year and during possibly the most critical moment of the game.

As a result, side judge Don Orr found himself in the swirled mess of fame that every official dreads. Suddenly, millions of NFL fans knew his name. Worse, they only knew him as the guy who missed calling what most viewers thought was an obvious touchdown, the same touchdown they watched over and over again in slow-motion.

Don Orr, however, was more than just that guy who stood in the spotlight that no official ever wants to stand. He wasn't just some guy who showed up at NFL headquarters and was handed a striped shirt with a yellow handkerchief. Orr's football roots ran deep and his road to standing on that field is rather compelling.

Orr grew up in Miami. Doctors diagnosed him with polio at age 14. He spent three months in the hospital and doctors wondered if he'd ever walk again.

Orr indeed walked again, and he also ran. Quite well, in fact.

He ran well enough that he played quarterback at Andrew Jackson High School. His play earned him scholarships to Florida, Miami, and Vanderbilt. Dartmouth recognized his academic skills and offered him an academic scholarship.

Orr chose Vanderbilt and led the Commodores to their first ever bowl victory – a 1955 Gator Bowl win over Auburn. He also played in the North-South collegiate all-star game, alternating at quarterback with Duke's soon-to-be legendary Sonny Jurgensen. George Halas took notice of Orr, and the Chicago Bears drafted Orr in the 1956 NFL Draft.

Orr joined the U.S. Army instead. He later built a career in Nashville, working for a machine company.

He started officiating high school football games. His college coach encouraged him to apply to officiate the Southeastern Conference. The SEC hired Orr. Later, an NFL officiating scout later asked him if he'd like to apply for a job with the NFL.

The league hired Orr in 1970. He spent 25 years as a league official and worked three Super Bowls: Super Bowls 17, 24, and 28.

The Oilers' task at hand for the moment was to make Super Bowl 14. The incompletion added weight to the task. Driving over 85 yards against the Steel Curtain in Pittsburgh and punching the ball in for a touchdown stood as a monumental achievement. Accomplishing that in the AFC Championship Game made it even more remarkable.

The Oilers had just scored one apparent touchdown. Repeating the task at Three Rivers Stadium required a steep climb, one more treacherous than most NFL teams could manage even with a second-and-goal situation.

Houston ran Tim Wilson on second down. Although he broke tackles from L.C. Greenwood and Dennis Winston, he managed only 2 yards.

The Steel Curtain swallowed the third-down play for a minimal gain.

The Oilers weren't even close enough to go for it on fourth down. They settled for a field goal on the first play of the fourth quarter.

Shortly afterward, during a time stoppage, one of the officials turned to Phil Tuckett. "I see you were filming over there in the end zone," he said. "Do you think we made the right call?"

Tuckett said everything happened so fast that it was tough to say. He told the official that if he had to make an immediate choice, he would say that they got the call right.

Either way, the Steelers still had the lead at home. Pittsburgh also pocketed a goal line stand to boost their morale. The Oilers overcame Pittsburgh's mammoth punt, but momentum didn't swing in their direction.

Although the Steelers clung to a mere 4-point lead, the difference between that and being tied going into the fourth quarter loomed large in the mental game, the confidence game, and the play calling. Pittsburgh could stay more conservative with the ball and the lead. Houston still needed to play a more liberal game of catchup.

CHAPTER 25

The Last Quarter Mile

Pittsburgh started the fourth quarter with their first first down of the second half. A holding call soon set the Steelers back, and Houston forced a third-and-20.

The Oiler defense played magnificently in the second half thus far, but Bradshaw rifled a pass to Swann at the Steeler 46, about a foot past the first-down marker. The Steelers won the game of inches on that play.

The Steelers also won the game of inches on their next third-down play. Franco Harris made a first down by the length of the ball. Bradshaw followed up that play with a pass to John Stallworth, putting the Steelers on Houston's 29.

Ideally, the Oilers needed to stop the Steelers from scoring. If Houston held the Steelers to a field goal, they remained in the game, but needed a touchdown to tie. If Pittsburgh scored a touchdown, that would put the Steelers ahead by 11. The Oilers rallied against

Washington for 11 points in the fourth quarter but duplicating that feat at Pittsburgh might prove next to impossible.

On first down, Rocky Bleier ran a trap play up the middle for 7 yards. The Oilers buckled up, however. Gregg Bingham hammered Franco Harris on a well-thrown pass on third down to knock the ball away. The incompletion forced a field goal attempt.

Matt Bahr's kick made it 20-13. Houston was still in the game.

On the previous drive, the Oilers proved they could move on Pittsburgh's defense. A touchdown drive here would tie the game deep in the fourth quarter.

The drive started disastrously on the kickoff. The ball skipped over returner Rich Ellender's shoulder. The Steelers attempted to recover inside the Oiler 15. Ellender swatted the ball out of bounds at the 11.

A penalty flag hit the turf and the officials huddled once more. Nearly a full minute later, Jim Tunney announced a 15-yard penalty against the Oilers for illegally batting the ball, with the penalty assessed on the rekick.

Steeler head coach Chuck Noll wanted to decline the penalty and keep the Oilers at their own 11. The officials again found themselves in a confusing situation without an easy answer.

After about another full minute, Tunney announced that Pittsburgh declined the penalty. Some officials still looked confused. A few players on both sides also appeared confused.

Three of the officials huddled again. Tunney entered the Oiler huddle to explain something. Eventually, the Oilers started the drive at the 11.

Houston lost a yard on first down. Nine minutes remained in the game. A screen to Wilson netted about 6 yards. That set up third-and-4.

Pastorini backpedaled and hit Rob Carpenter over the middle. Carpenter made it across the 30 for a first down. The Oilers had a real chance to build a drive.

The clock showed under seven minutes remaining on Houston's next third down. Pastorini fired a strike over the middle for a completion near midfield.

Guido Merkens turned to run with Mel Blount draped around him. Ron Johnson crashed in with a helmet-to-helmet hit. Merkens fumbled, and the Steelers recovered at Houston's 45. Merkens was injured on the play and needed help off the field.

The clock slid under five minutes. Houston's defense needed an immediate stop to force a punt. On third down, however, Rocky Bleier made a diving catch at Houston's 18 for a first down.

The play marked the 10th third down conversion for the Steelers, compared to 3 for Houston.

Houston forced a third-and-2 at the two-minute warning. Holding Pittsburgh to a field goal held a small ray of hope for a quick score and an onside kick.

The sun faded on Houston's season, however. The Steelers made the first down.

The clock kept ticking.

The Oiler defense didn't quit. They forced another third down on the 4-yard line with under a minute left, but Rocky Bleier took the ball over the goal line for a Steeler touchdown and a 27-13 victory.

The Steelers punched their ticket to Super Bowl 14. The Oiler dream vanished into the frigid ether of the Pennsylvania winter.

A mass of fans congregated on the field as the teams departed toward their respective locker rooms. Joe Greene and Steeler defensive end John Banaszak both sought out Dan Pastroini. Each put their arm around him with words of encouragement.

Here's what Dan remembers: "Joe Greene was telling me, 'You hang your head up.' He said, 'You beat us today. You know it and we know it. God bless you and you walk out of here with your head high.'

"I reached over and tapped him on the helmet and said, 'Go win it for our division.'

"And they did."

CHAPTER 26

The Journey Domeward

Twenty-eight teams dreamed of playing that Sunday when they reported to training camp in the hot summer of 1979. The Oilers won their way into being one of the four teams playing in conference championships. Yet nobody wanted to be in the Oilers position now. The physical and emotional pain from the loss churned from disbelief to chilling reality.

Houston knew they could beat Pittsburgh. The Steelers knew the Oilers could beat them. And yet, despite the possibilities that lasted well into the fourth quarter, the finality of the result sank into the bones of each player.

Houston fell one game short of the red, white, and Columbia blue championship dream two years in a row. The current loss thrust the Oilers back to square one, into the off-season, then to training camp, then to having to prove themselves again in the regular season, fighting pain and fearsome opponent, only to land shy of the ultimate goal, in the same heap as the 27 other NFL teams whose season ended with a devastating loss or a brutal exclusion from the playoff dance.

Elvin Bethea's stomach stung under the cruel reality of the loss.

He also deeply understood that Houston's back-to-back runs to the AFC Championship Game were a thing of beauty, grit, and accomplishment. His beloved coach and band of brothers journeyed together and touched a plateau just shy of the mountain top, yet with a view and experience that few obtain.

Bethea knew after twelve years in the National Football League that his football days were numbered. He knew the magic and success of 1979 wasn't something you could draw up on a chalkboard and easily replicate the next year. The warrior removed his helmet and suffered the aches of physical pain and heartbreaking loss in the cold, stark confines of the Oiler locker room.

"That was our last run. When we came in at the end of the game I just sat down in front of my locker and I actually cried. I said to myself, 'This is it. We'll never see another year like this.'

"I looked at my locker and said, 'This is my last shot getting close to the Super Bowl.' And I knew that."

His tears did not fall alone. Each player felt the bleak pain of pressing to less than one quarter of football away from playing in Super Bowl 14 only to rapidly descend into the aftermath of losing within a matter of minutes.

Athletes have trainers and techniques to prevail over physical pain. Playbooks and fundamentals guide players to victory over opponents. Emotional pain offers neither playbook nor special brace for relief. You can tape a broken bone, but you can't tape a broken heart.

Each individual stood forced to deal with defeat's agony, their feelings and experiences ensconced solely within their own memories, their own minds, their own souls. Some asked themselves, "What if I would have made just one more play?"

The dream that robustly burned only one week before in San Diego, with a flame so searing that every Oiler fan and player felt its realness, now lay stilled, reduced to cold, smoky ashes without hope of reigniting.

The Oiler equipment managers and logistics team carried out their own sullen tasks. They gathered shoulder pads and jerseys, and packed helmets and cleats for the long plane ride home. They organized players and coaches onto the bus, to the airport, and onto the plane back home to Houston.

The team boarded the plane and headed home. Bum Phillips reminded them that they were going to the Astrodome after they landed, for another Domecoming welcome from the fans.

Dan Pastorini chose a seat in the back of the plane. Like many a man heartbroken from a loss in love or career, he turned to drowning his sorrows. Bum Phillips got up from his seat. He shook hands and individually spoke to the players.

Pastorini recalls what Phillips said to him.

"He comes and he faces me. He grabs me by the shoulders, looks me in the eye like a son and he said, 'Daniel, you're a warrior and I love you.'

"I said, 'Thanks, Bum.'

"And then he said, 'Do you still feel the same way as you did last year?'"

Phillips was talking about the conversation the two had during the off-season, when Pastorini told Phillips that if he was holding the team back, to trade him. Phillips had told Dan that he didn't want to trade him and to put all his effort into the 1979 season. If Pastorini felt the same way after the season, Bum said he would trade him anywhere he wanted.

Pastorini recalled answering Phillips' question on the plane: "I'm sitting there. I had totally forgotten about that conversation. I was stumped on what he meant. And I'm searching, searching, searching. Then I thought, 'Oh my God. I guess he does want to trade me. I guess I am the problem.' It all came back to me.

"And I go, 'Well, yeah, I guess so.'

"And he goes, "Alright. You're a man of your word. You gave me your all, you stuck it out, where do you want to go?'

"I said, "I guess the West Coast.""

The plane landed in Houston and the team boarded busses to the Astrodome. Only Bum Phillips and Dan Pastorini knew that Pastorini had played his last game as a Houston Oiler.

The team busses pulled away from the airport and the players couldn't believe their eyes.

Fans lined the streets all the way to the Astrodome with Luv Ya Blue signs and showered support upon a team that just lost the 1979 AFC Championship Game. Fans waited in the Astrodome for at least an hour before the team arrived. Many walked a half mile or more from their cars to the Astrodome. Parked cars lined the streets.

The busses pulled into the Astrodome parking lot. Thousands of fans gathered outside of the stadium in the lot. The team rolled into the Astrodome packed with jubilant fans. Combined with the parking lots, crowd estimates stood between 60-80,000 people. Those numbers topped the record-setting attendance at Three Rivers Stadium for the AFC Championship.

Pastorini and Earl Campbell thundered around the Astrodome turf on police motorcycles. Robert Brazile and Vernon Perry rode on the backs of horses.

Brazile remembered how blown away he was by the event being even bigger than the previous season. "The whole city stopped what they were doing to cheer a team that they loved and cherished during that time, which was the Houston Oilers," Brazile said. "I had never seen that many people in the Astrodome. I had never seen that many people on the outskirts, on the freeways, blowing, honking, cheering us on like we had won a game."

The celebration gave Curley Culp goose bumps. "Yeah, it was wild," the Hall of Famer said. "It was a great feeling. It gave me goose pimples to feel that kind of love from a group of fans that really shared in the kind of work we did on the football field."

A makeshift stage provided a platform with a microphone with which the players spoke to the crowd. "Houston Oilers Number One" played through the Astrodome's sound system. The Luv Ya Blue crowd sang and danced with pom-poms and signs. They cheered as loudly as they would for a game-winning touchdown.

Bum Phillips felt overwhelmed. He got lost in the moment. He stepped up to the microphone and uttered perhaps his most famous phrase, "Last year we knocked on the door. This year we beat on it. Next year we're going to kick the son-of-a-bitch in!"

The crowd lost its mind. Fans went completely berserk. Houston loved Bum Phillips and they loved the Oilers.

Phillips later apologized for the comment, saying his mother taught him not to speak like that in front of women and children.

People often wonder what makes a town so fanatical that 70,000 or more people crammed into a stadium to greet a team that lost a game. By comparison, an estimated 3,000 people gathered to greet the Los Angeles Rams after they won the NFC Championship for a spot in Super Bowl 14.

You'd be hard pressed to find anything in sports history comparable to the Luv Ya Blue spectacle and the fans. It is easy to look at the surface and say people turned out to support a team that lost, but fans in the Astrodome that night celebrated more than the events on January 6, 1980, the day of the 1979 AFC Championship Game.

Perhaps the city of Houston didn't focus on the loss at Pittsburgh, but rather on what the Oilers had won. The Oilers won the love of an entire city and showcased that city on nationally televised games. The exposure amplified the awareness of Houston's growth and identity throughout the country.

The Oilers won the respect and hearts of NFL fans everywhere, especially those who love cheering for the gritty underdog. The Oilers also won the respect of the Pittsburgh Steelers, recognized as the team of the 1970s.

Furthermore, the Oilers won the right to say that they never quit and never let their teammates down. They earned the right to look at themselves in the mirror 40 years later and truthfully tell themselves that when everything mattered, they never held back and never quit. Everything inside of them -- their will, their determination, their fighting spirit -- was left on the field.

While the Houston Oilers didn't win Super 14, the 1979 AFC Championship Game, nor incredibly even a division title, they were champions of a city and champions of each other. The team melded a bond that can't be conveyed through record books and online databases, only curated within the hearts of those who witnessed it and experienced the Luv Ya Blue phenomenon during 1979 Houston Oilers season.

The Steelers eventually won Super Bowl 14 over the Rams. The Renfro Play stayed a big story as Super Bowl Sunday approached. The play likely pushed the NFL into making replay part of the game much sooner than if the play had never happened.

Players from both the Steelers and Oilers answered questions about the call after the game. Cornerback Ron Johnson said he didn't think that Renfro caught the ball when the play occurred. After he saw the replay, however, he said the play looked much closer than he originally believed.

Sports Illustrated quoted Joe Greene as saying the call bothered him because some people would question the Steeler victory. He wanted fans and media to fully respect the game's outcome and didn't appreciate the call adding an element of people saying, "Yeah, they won. But the call ruined it for Houston."

Lynn Swann said he found it unfortunate that the call obscured the fact that both teams played a hard-fought game. He added that if writers and fans wanted to question the Steeler win, then they also needed to recognize that Pittsburgh scored 10 points in the fourth quarter, caused a turnover, and likely would have responded in similar fashion had the play been ruled a touchdown. The Steelers had won three Super Bowls and a lot of tight playoff games along that championship highway before that game. They knew how to win when the games mattered most.

Historical stats back up Swann's statement. In 1979, Pittsburgh outscored opponents in the fourth quarter by nearly 100 points. The 1979 AFC Championship Game win marked 16 straight home wins for the Steelers, and 23 out of 24. During their run of 4 championships in 6 seasons, the Steelers only lost one home game after leading or tied going into the fourth quarter.

In the 1970s, the Steelers only lost one playoff game at home – and that was to the 1972 Miami Dolphins, the only team in the playoff era to go undefeated through the regular season and the playoffs.

NBC devoted much of their 1979 AFC Championship Game postgame coverage to the Renfro Play. The locker room reporter peppered Steeler coach Chuck Noll with questions about the play on live television. The network also broadcasted an interview with the only reporter allowed to speak to the officials, a local writer named Vito Stellino.

Stellino explained that side judge Don Orr questioned whether Renfro had possession of the ball before he slid out of bounds. He said the officials huddled and nobody claimed to have a better view.

Therefore, they all sided with Orr's concerns and ruled the pass incomplete.

NBC showed the video replay several times during the postgame, showing angles that clearly put that ruling under suspicion. The postgame show's host, Bryant Gumbel, continued to criticize the call. The play grabbed the majority of the postgame show's attention.

Sports Illustrated pointed out that the referee's Jim Tunney's hand signal of "incomplete" differed from the official signal that indicated a player juggled the ball and that possession was questioned. Tunney gave the standard incomplete sign when he made the call. He didn't use the alternating arm motions that signaled a receiver didn't have possession of the ball.

The Oilers, their fans, and the Houston media obviously didn't like the officials' decision. A lot of ink and airtime lambasted both the call and the NFL rules that prohibited referees from using replay. Bum Phillips told reporters that Oiler game film not only showed that Renfro caught the ball but that the Steelers also committed pass interference on the play.

Dan Pastorini said in the documentary *We Were the Oilers: The Luv Ya Blue Era!* that he liked the Oilers' chances in a tie game against Pittsburgh going into the fourth quarter. Like Swann's previously stated point, history also grants Pastorini's thoughts credence.

The Houston Oilers, with Pastorini at quarterback, stood as the only team to beat Pittsburgh at home over the 1978 and '79 seasons. The Oilers were one of only two teams to beat Pittsburgh at home twice during their Super Bowl runs. They were the only AFC Central team to beat Pittsburgh at all in Three Rivers Stadium since it opened in 1970.

Additionally, Pastorini was the only NFL quarterback to take a team that was either tied or behind going into the fourth quarter against Pittsburgh and beat the Steelers at home during that timeframe. That happened in 1974, the season the Steelers won Super Bowl 9. The teams entered the fourth quarter tied at 10, and the Oilers prevailed by a field goal.

The 1979 Oilers also conjured up the magic and grit that made a road win against Pittsburgh possible. The Dallas game proved that point. So did the playoff win at San Diego. Pittsburgh owned the stats that day, but Houston had a knack for losing games on the stat sheet but winning them on the scoreboard.

That said, had the Renfro Play stood as a touchdown the result merely would have improved the Oilers' chances of winning. The Steelers still held home field advantage and several Hall of Famers dotted their roster on both sides of the ball. A steep climb remained to beat them at home, even with momentum going into the fourth quarter and the flexibility to better balance their offense.

Perhaps Bum Phillips said it best when he said, "We still had 59 more minutes to beat Pittsburgh."

Pittsburgh's monumental stand after the Oilers recovered a fumbled punt may have contributed more to the Steeler win than an official's call. The Oilers also gave up three turnovers. The Steelers held Earl Campbell to 15 yards on 17 attempts. Although Houston held a slight edge in net passing yards, the Steelers outgained Houston by more than the length of a football field in total yards.

Football isn't a game won and lost on a single play and the Oilers players would be the first to tell you that. It's true that certain plays turn out to be more important than others, but several important plays happen in each game.

Side judge Don Orr has since been quoted as saying that he wishes that the NFL approved the usage of instant replay before all eyes turned to him at the end of the third quarter of the AFC Championship. He and the rest of the crew could have made the call and that would have been it. Replay would have either confirmed the call or overturned it. The likelihood of the play still being discussed

40 years later would be remote, and it certainly would have saved him a lot of unwanted attention at the time.

Two things were lost on the Renfro Play, and both kind of intertwine with each other.

NFL fans lost the chance to see the AFC champion decided in an even up fifteen-minute battle between arguably the two best teams in pro football.

The two teams lost an opportunity to prove what would happen in such a setting. Would Houston find a way to grind out a gutty type of win like those gained at Miami, Dallas, and San Diego, or the ones the Oilers pulled out at Three Rivers in 1974 and 1978?

Or would the Steelers have responded exactly the same as they did with the 4-point lead -- by scoring, getting a turnover, and scoring again?

Those questions remain answered only in theory.

Phil Tuckett developed his film after the game. The film included the reverse angle he captured of the Renfro Play. The NFL released word that the angle validated the official's call on the play after the film was developed. Today, Tuckett maintains that the angle conclusively raises the question of possession, and he still agrees with the on-the-spot call.

He adds that he also was at the Immaculate Reception game, and that NFL Films had twenty-two cameras at the game. They froze all twenty-two angles of the play and still couldn't decide whether or not Franco Harris actually caught the ball.

Tuckett believes that the Renfro Play is more definitive from the reverse angle.

Although many people agree with him, many people also agree that it was a catch based on their observations. Forty years later, the Renfro Play is almost always listed as one of the most controversial calls in NFL history.

Pete Rozelle feared that using replay would raise more questions than answers.

Would the Renfro Play call stand under today's replay rules? What if the play had been called a touchdown, would it still have been controversial? Would Houston have pulled out a magical win or would the champion Steelers have crushed the rally?

Forty years later, more questions than answers surround a play that took only a split second to run.

Perhaps the only thing everyone can agree upon is that to see the Houston-Pittsburgh rivalry come down to fifteen minutes, champion versus tenacious underdog, throwing every last punch they knew for a trip to Super Bowl 14, would have been amazing to watch.

PART 6
A NEW DECADE AND NEW DESTINATIONS

CHAPTER 27

The Sun Rises and Also Sets

The 1980s chimed in less than a week before the 1979 AFC Championship Game. The Oiler family experienced great changes in the new decade.

Bum Phillips worked out a trade with Al Davis and the Oakland Raiders. The Oilers sent Dan Pastorini to Oakland straight up for Ken Stabler.

Stabler, coincidentally, was the only other quarterback to beat the Steelers in Pittsburgh twice during the six-year span in which Pittsburgh won four Super Bowls.

Pastorini believes that his big day against Oakland in the 1979 regular season roused the Raiders' interest in him and that was a strong factor in the deal.

The trade took the NFL by storm. Two teams exchanged their franchise quarterbacks. Nobody knew what to expect.

Quarterbacks were synonymous with their teams during the 1970s. Terry Bradshaw, Dan Fouts, Roger Staubach, Joe Ferguson,

Jim Hart, Ken Anderson. Football fans knew who they were and what team they quarterbacked. Pastorini and the Oilers went together like peanut butter and jelly, even a casual fan's vocabulary.

The teams announced the trade in March.

Much of the Houston media wasn't especially kind to Pastorini. One reporter traversed the Houston bar circuit and claimed to have only found a handful of people who wanted to see Pastorini remain as the Oilers' quarterback. The writer quoted one person as saying that Stabler would make the Oilers a winning team – this after the Oilers made two straight AFC Championship Game appearances.

Another headline said that Pastorini was both the most successful and least successful quarterback in franchise history.

The reaction to the trade illustrated the relationship fans and the media had with Pastorini – some loved him one minute and hated him the next. Some adored him all the time. Others despised him no matter how well he performed. A lot of that comes with the job of being a big-league quarterback.

The media and the public didn't know the trade's backstory. Some guessed the Oilers traded him because of his contract. Others guessed a divide occurred when the team told Pastorini they didn't want him racing dragsters in the offseason. A few speculated that owner Bud Adams ordered the trade.

Pastorini packed to replace a legend in Oakland.

Stabler said he couldn't be happier coming to the Oilers, and Oiler fans liked the thought of having a quarterback who had won a Super Bowl.

Many Oiler fans and Houston writers thought they now had a team that could beat Pittsburgh in the playoffs. Sports writers throughout the country evaluated the deal and most kept a wait-and-see attitude since Stabler was 34 years old and Pastorini, 30.

Pastorini started the first five games for the Raiders in 1980. He suffered a broken leg in Week 5. The Raiders were 2-2 at the time. Pastorini never played another regular season down for Oakland.

Stabler led the Oilers to an identical record in 1980, 11-5. Ironically, the record placed them in a wildcard game at Oakland. The Raiders won, 27-7, en route to winning Super Bowl 15.

Pastorini didn't really feel like he was a part of the Raider family like the brotherhood he felt in Houston. He covers a lot of that in his book, *Taking Flak*. He joined the Raiders on the sidelines during Super Bowl 15 but didn't play.

Moments after the 1979 AFC Championship Game at Pittsburgh, NBC interviewed Pastorini live on national television. He spoke softly and sullen, obviously deeply hurt by the loss. He said that the loss was a tough pill to swallow but there was always another chance somewhere.

A year later he stood on the winning sidelines at the Super Bowl. It truly was another time and another place. He wasn't a Houston Oiler. He suffered a broken leg and lost his starting job. He was miserable. He finally had his coveted Super Bowl ring but gave it away to a charity.

In January of 1979, he was the starting quarterback for one of the best teams in pro football. A year later, he was out of a job.

Bum Phillips followed a similar trajectory. He led the Oilers to an 11-5 record in 1980 and a wildcard berth. Shortly after the wildcard loss to Oakland, the Oilers fired Phillips as head coach. Houston sports writers still call it, "The New Year's Eve Massacre."

In January of 1979, Bum Phillips stood as head coach of one of the finest teams in pro football. A year later, he too was out of a job.

The New Orleans Saints hired Phillips for the 1981 season. Earl Campbell, Tim Wilson, Leon Gray, Ken Stabler, and others eventually followed Bum from Houston to New Orleans. Phillips never recreated the Luv Ya Blue magic in The Big Easy. He mostly endured losing seasons.

The Raiders released Pastorini just before the 1981 regular season. He spent a season a piece on the Rams roster and on the Eagles roster. Like Phillips, Pastorini's career peaked with the Luv Ya Blue era Oilers.

The Houston Oilers also peaked with Bum, Dan, and the Luv Ya Blue brotherhood. The team made the AFC Championship Game in 1978 and 1979. The Houston Oilers never returned to the AFC Championship Game.

In 1981, the Oilers suffered their first of several losing seasons in a row. The San Francisco 49ers and Cincinnati Bengals, two doormats of the 1979 season, met in Super Bowl 16 to determine the 1981 NFL champion.

In just two years, the Oilers swung from back-to-back AFC Championship Game appearances to the first of several losing seasons. Bum Phillips went from coaching one of the best teams in the NFL to coaching one of the worst. Dan Pastorini went from being a star quarterback fading back to pass to fading away as an NFL player.

On the afternoon of January 6, 1980, the Oilers held a 10-3 second-quarter lead at Pittsburgh. Dan Pastorini had yet to throw an incompletion against one of the best defenses in NFL history. Bum Phillips stood coaching on the sidelines, a week after he coaxed out one of the most remarkable victories in franchise history at San Diego.

Yet by January of 1981, Pastorini and Phillips were gone. By January of 1982, the Oilers' winning ways had disappeared. By January of 1997, just 15 years later, the Houston Oilers were on their way to Tennessee to eventually become the Tennessee Titans.

PART 7
POSTGAME WRAP UP

CHAPTER 28

Reflecting on the Scrapbook

Dan Pastorini has a lot in common with many of us. He once dreamed of playing in the NFL and quarterbacking his team to victory like his childhood heroes Bart Starr, Johnny Unitas, Daryle Lamonica, and John Brodie. The difference is that a large portion of his NFL dreams came true, more than most of us kids who picked up a football pretending to be our favorite players.

Pastorini remembers standing on the field in the Astrodome before a preseason game as Bart Starr stood wearing his famous number 15 jersey on the opposing sidelines. Pastorini realized his life led him to a place where his heroes were now his peers. He stood where they stood.

That place, lined up behind center as a franchise quarterback, also lined him up in the spotlight underneath a magnifying glass. Every pass and every third-down play call in every game came with commentary from broadcasters, reporters, people watching from the stands, and fans watching on television. Every experience with the public, from going out to dinner, to being asked for a favor by a charity, to having a few drinks at the corner bar garnered extra attention.

A lot of young people who experience success or nudge alongside their dreams make mistakes. A lot of us make decisions that adversely affect our future and we'd love to have a do-over. We're all human, and we all do things that we regret later. Sometimes we can fix it, sometimes we can't.

At one time, Dan Pastorini was a young man, a star quarterback, and popular with some of the most desirable women of the 1970s like Farrah Fawcett and June Wilkinson. He also had money, nowhere near even what today's NFL minimum salary is, but still a fair amount for a guy in his 20s during the 1970s. He had fame. His actions on and off the field danced in the spotlight, complete with fans and harsh critics alike. He did what a lot of us might do in that situation – he did a lot of things he's not proud of, and a lot of things he'd do differently today.

One of the biggest regrets he has, if not the biggest, is leaving Houston. Bum Phillips also regretted the trade and called it one of his biggest mistakes.

Pastorini wondered why Phillips asked him about a trade on the flight home after the 1979 AFC Championship Game. Leaving Houston was the last thing on Pastorini's mind during those painful hours after the game. Pastorini couldn't believe everything happened so fast – Phillips worked out preliminary aspects of the deal within weeks.

Dan gave his all to the Oilers. He played hurt and refused to quit even when trailing by more than 20 points. He strongly supported Gifford Nielsen when Nielsen played in games. The way things went down so quickly and during such painful and confusing moments after the loss bothered Pastorini for a long time.

Years after it was all said and done, he and Phillips talked about it at Bum's ranch.

Pastorini remembers: "Years later, we were down at his ranch riding around. I said, 'I got to ask you something. Why did you ask me that on the plane going back?'

"He said, 'Dan, I didn't think you'd say yes.'

"And he said, 'What I should have said was, 'Screw you, I ain't trading you.'

"I said, 'I wish you had. I really wish you had. Because I would have loved to have finished my career here with you.'"

Both Phillips and Pastorini lived up to their word.

In this case, Phillips promised himself he'd never deny a player's request to be traded and told Pastorini he'd trade him if his feelings didn't change with the 1979 season.

Pastorini wishes he never spoke about his concerns about holding the team back after the 1978 AFC Championship Game. He now calls the trade a gentlemen's agreement between two men who let foolish pride dictate an outcome that neither wanted to see.

Again, many of us can relate. We've allowed our pride, doubt, or fears influence the way things turned out, sometimes even on the verge of a dream coming true. We look back and wish we would have taken a different path. The biggest difference between Dan Pastorini and a lot of us is that his regrets were performed on the NFL's brightly lit stage.

A lot of people turn bitter after they touched the golden lantern, rubbed it the wrong way, and asked the genie for the wrong wish. Some point the finger and blame others. Some let the hurt drag them down into longstanding bitterness, anger, or self-loathing.

Others move forward. Like in his playing days, Dan's pressed on. He took the best he could from the past and hasn't let the past get the best of him. He is grateful that he competed at the highest level and made lifelong friends as a result.

The Houston Oilers were family on the field during the 1979 season and remain like family off the field. Robert Brazile sums up how the team remains a family today.

"When you say Houston Oilers, you're talking about the Luv Ya Blue family," Brazile said. "A lot of people don't realize what we did as a group and what we're still doing. We still communicate with each other. We still care about each other."

Robert also greatly appreciates how the Titans organization honors the Luv Ya Blue family and how owner Amy Adams added his name to the franchise's Ring of Honor.

The Luv Ya Blue family bonded as a band of brothers in the primes of their lives. All were in their 20s or early 30s with premier athletic skills, rising to the top of the National Football League while coming of age as players, fathers, and men.

Rich Caster looks back fondly on that period of his life. "I can say that the three years that I spent in Houston with the Oilers were the best years that I can remember in my life," Caster said. "That's not only playing football. That's everything I was doing. I was starting my family and everything. Houston Oilers, Luv Ya Blue, I just love the atmosphere and love being associated with the Luv Ya Blue legacy."

The 1979 Houston Oilers season emulated a heroic journey of valor, victory, joy, adversity, and ultimately a defeat one game shy of the ultimate goal. The road proved rugged, rewarding, dangerous, and richly memorable.

In sports and in life, dreams hurl themselves toward the stars while gathering roots deep within our hearts. Each step, each yard, each gain nudges us closer to our destinations.

Some gains are easy, like a Pastorini toss to a wide-open Ken Burrough downfield, or a swing pass to Tim Wilson with Carl Mauck and Leon Gray in front with a clear path to the end zone.

Others prove much more difficult like Earl Campbell breaking tackles to pick up a first down or Elvin Bethea fighting off two blockers to make a drive-ending sack.

Adversity strikes like a thigh bruise, a wounded throwing arm, or Joe Greene breaking through the line. Life isn't always fair, much like a touchdown erased by circumstance, a shot taken out of bounds into the first down marker, or a critic's static occluding a fan's cheers. A torn ACL can end an athlete's season much like a torn trust can end our own dreams.

For a lot of us, many dreams indeed fade much like the dreams of most NFL teams – falling short of the ultimate goal. For the 1979 Houston Oilers, the ultimate goal was winning Super Bowl 14.

The road the Oilers traveled wasn't as easy as looking at the season schedule, predicting wins and assuming all would go as planned. The same often goes for those of us pulling out a notebook or calendar and enthusiastically writing out our goals and plans.

In the NFL, only one team achieves their ultimate goal each year. In life, we often leave more dreams unfinished than realized.

The unexpected always arrives unannounced. Sometimes the unexpected helps, like a late John Riggins fumble helped the Oilers in Week 1. Sometimes the unexpected tosses you for a loss, like Billy "White Shoes" Johnson being lost for the whole season in Week 2 or Ken Burrough being banged up for the playoffs. Sometimes the unexpected brings out the best in you, like making four interceptions and blocking a field goal after your star teammates are injured.

The 1979 Oilers overcame large point deficits to win and narrowly escaped defeat with late interceptions and field goals. The team routed a few opponents, and got routed themselves a couple of times.

There were losses in each game. Sometimes those losses were measured in yards, sometimes in points, but each loss left the team ready to go on the next play, eager to pick up the pieces of lost yardage, regain the lead, or move on to the next game.

Each game also brought celebrations. Celebrations of touchdowns, first downs, field goals and defensive celebrations for sacks, interceptions, and fumble recoveries. Waves of pom-poms and explosions of cheers rocked the Astrodome during home games. Surges of excitement beamed through television sets and radios when the Oilers were on the road.

The red, white, and Columbia blue oil tanker sank in the Port of Pittsburgh en route to Super Bowl 14. The loss ended the dream and journey that the 1979 Houston Oilers shared with fans in Houston and across America. Each player and each fan suffered the heartbreak of loss and the dashing of hopes.

Years later, washed ashore, stood the lasting treasures of memories, friendships, joy, triumphs through adversity, and the communal spirits of team and family. For those willing to dig through the sands of time and ashes of lost hopes, remnants of loss transformed into glory, stories of disappointment morphed into tales of triumph, and sentimental wisps of experience calmed the waters where bitter tears once flowed.

Much like the 1979 Houston Oilers, we line up and run the plays of life the best we can. Sometimes we end up going further than it may have looked possible at points along the trail, and sometimes our paths look like a busted play that lost 15 yards.

When a dream's run ends, we may not wind up at the place that our maps and charts told us was the ultimate destination. Yet, over time, we reach into our satchels and find forgotten gemstones that we collected along the way, reminding us that it's not necessarily where the journey ended that matters, but rather the person we became and the friends and memories we made along the way.

Acknowledgements

A very special thank you to the Houston Oiler players who interviewed for this book. I greatly appreciate all of you and the time you spent sharing stories and information. Many of you I've gotten to know beforehand through *The Game before the Money* and/or *We Were the Oilers: The Luv Ya Blue Era!*. It is always a special day when I get to chat with any of you and for those of you that I got to speak with for the very first time, I really enjoyed our time together.

My individual thanks go to Willie Alexander, Mike Barber, Elvin Bethea, Gregg Bingham, Robert Brazile, Ken Burrough, Rich Caster, Curley Culp, Andy Dorris, Billy "White Shoes" Johnson, Carl Mauck, Dan Pastorini, Vernon Perry, and Mike Stensrud.

Coach Ed Biles passed away before the book was published. I greatly appreciated his great sense of joy and the time he spent sharing his memories. I hope that this book honors his memory in some small way.

Several others deserve a great deal of thanks. Mickey Herskowitz (quite possibly the greatest storyteller of our time) and John McClain, thank you for your priceless insight about those times and that era from your perspectives. I would also like to thank Debbie Phillips who has always been so supportive of my wife and me.

Thanks also to Lee Ofman for sharing the fun story of how "Houston Oilers Number One" rose to life, and to Phil Tuckett for his outstanding stories about Bum Phillips and relating his on-the-field experience during one of the most important moments in franchise history.

A thank you also goes out to Gow Media and Craig Larson for inspiring this project, as well as Fred Faour, and Andrew Carlson for bringing it to fruition in its first incarnation.

An extra special thanks to my wife, Lisa, for her always encouraging my work and lighting up my days brighter than any scoreboard.

Thanks are also in order for the Texas Public Library system. Specific thanks are due to public libraries in Dallas, San Antonio, Houston, New Braunfels, and Schertz.

I would be remiss in forgetting to thank our dog, Lambeau, who dutifully napped by my side as I researched and typed away at my keyboard.

About the Author

Jackson Michael's given name is actually Michael Jackson. You may have heard of someone else with that name. Hence, the thinly-veiled pen name.

Michael works as an oral historian, author, audio engineer, and musician. He lives in Texas with his wife and their very athletic terrier-schnauzer mix named Lambeau.

He loved watching sports at an early age and has followed the NFL since the late 1970s, at the height of the Luv Ya Blue phenomenon.

Other works by Jackson Michael:

Book: *The Game Before the Money: Voices of the Men Who Built the NFL*

Film/DVD: *We Were the Oilers: The Luv Ya Blue Era!*

Podcasts: *The Game before the Money Podcast*

          The Texas Sports Hall of Fame Podcast

For more information, please visit TheGameBeforeTheMoney.com

Social Media: Facebook Page: TheGameBeforeTheMoney

Twitter: @GameBeforeMoney

Instagram: @GameBeforeMoney

www.ingramcontent.com/pod-product-compliance
Lightning Source LLC
Chambersburg PA
CBHW072151100526
44589CB00015B/2187